Denied by Allah

NOOR ZAHEER

Vitasta
Let Knowledge Spread

Published by
Renu Kaul Verma for
Vitasta Publishing Pvt Ltd
2/15, Ansari Road, Daryaganj
New Delhi - 110 002
info@vitastapublishing.com

ISBN 978-93-82711-58-2

First Edition 2015
2nd Reprint 2019
MRP ₹250

Typeset & Cover Design by Vits Press
Cover illustration by Babli Das
Printed by Vikas Computer and Printers

CONTENTS

The worst kind of battle is the one not confronted.
This book is dedicated to those who dare to question.

ACKNOWLEDGEMENT

When I look back, it is hard to think of a reason why these women opened their hearts to me, trusted me with their dark secrets, allowed me entry into the painful, bleak portions of their lives, and let me probe the fine crevices of their minds. I am grateful to them for sharing something so personal, knowing that I was going to make it public. I am grateful to them for allowing me to wage their battle. Their names have, however, been changed to protect their privacy.

My three children have grown up witnessing my mood swings and writer's blocks. This book, however, was like testing the angels as I emerged from one depression to sink into another, deeper one. Thank you dears for understanding that I could not explain or give reasons for the humiliation each case study brought with it. And thanks for keeping me supplied with endless cups of coffee in the middle of the night.

Every author believes that what she has written is the final word and hence sacrosanct. My grateful thanks to my editor Veena Batra for very patiently bearing with my tantrums and making me understand that it is not the size of the chapter but the precision of the words that would add weight to the text.

A very dear and undemanding friend, a thank you is due to Renu Kaul Verma, Managing Director, Vitasta Publishing Pvt Ltd, for accepting the concept of the book and for prodding me with emails and phone calls to complete the book. But more than that for having the courage to stand by me to publish a book on a subject that has never been discussed.

Though a lot of information is now available on the internet, I have relied in the translations of the *Quran* by Syed Yusuf Ali and M Marmaduke Pickthall.

Throughout the process of researching and writing this book, Comrade Mohammad Mehdi encouraged and guided me, his pet line being, "I am only a phone call away." It is my misfortune that he passed away in December 2014 before the book could be out.

I have long admired Babli Das as a painter and watched her grow as an artist. I am grateful to her for sharing a painting from her 'Woman' series to be used as the cover of the book.

AUTHOR'S NOTE

When I read out some portions of this book to a few friends they said that it was an ill-timed attack on Islam. And why did I, a writer of fiction, wish to write about Halala and other indignities that Muslim women are subjected to in the name of religion?

What is Halala? After divorcing his wife, if a man regrets his decision and wants the woman back as his wife, he cannot simply marry her again. She first has to be married to someone else, divorced or widowed, and then only would she be 'halal' for the first man. This second, 'short-term marriage' is usually paid for with the understanding that a divorce would happen soon, usually after the nuptial night.

I had first heard about the increase in the Halala cases about ten years ago while attending a *Jansunvai* (public hearing) in Badayun, Uttar Pradesh.

When I narrated these incidents to my elder sister, her immediate reaction was: 'What lies! Of course it doesn't happen like this. Islam is a woman-friendly religion.' So firm was her conviction that I had second thoughts about the validity of the entire event and even my own reaction. It was the sheer recurrence of similar incidents that brought me back to the problem, leading to several interviews, discussions and public hearings.

Why hasn't the issue been highlighted before? Why is this and so many other crimes committed in the name of religion, never openly discussed? Discussions with Muslim scholars made me aware of the sharp economic divide. Not that divorces do not happen amongst the rich; but the women are usually strong enough, socially and economically, and have family support if a divorce takes place. She either has the children with her or has visiting rights. She also does not suffer the same humiliation after talaq, perhaps because the majority of the upper middle class Muslims have a liberal progressive attitude.

But they do not support any movement against these archaic laws, or openly condemn them or even give them a thought. Why? They too have read the *Quran* and the Hadith and are aware of these issues.

Every time I have tried to discuss the *Quran*, Hadith or the Shariah in secular, democratic platforms, I have been told that these discussions should be held within the Muslim community and any change has to be initiated by Muslim scholars. I disagree. The wider the discussion, the more embarrassment it would cause to people who are comfortable in letting things remain as they are for the Muslim women.

Some sociologists and activists advised that I should not base the book on case studies or make it 'story-centric'. It would water down the effect.

But I am basically a writer of fiction, and nothing I say, write or discuss, is complete without a story. I also believe that fiction does not grow out of nothing; at its root is stark reality.

Often friends inquired if a case study, written as fiction, could replace a serious discussion on law? Would it hold against the onslaught of formal advocacy? My contention is that it will. Mere statistics, data, facts, laws pale when faced by the stark stories of down to earth reality. Facts recorded or dictated in books are hugely different from what is happening in reality. These tales narrate that difference.

Stories are a great medium for change. History has time and again proved the importance of folklore, Jataka tales, stories of fairyland, the supernatural and stories of valour and chivalry. It is from stories that human values are inculcated in the character of a person—teaching one the choices to be made and the struggles to be supported.

Statistical numbers don't usually motivate us to stand up for change and to empathize with the victims.

Most Muslim families engage a Hafiz or send their children to the local madrasa to read the *Quran*. The purpose of every woman knowing the *Quran* and reading it once before marriage is that she should know not only the process of worship but also the law. However, the Muslim Personal Law falls amongst the things that are never told or discussed. Every single meeting of Muslim women that I have attended has always ended with women saying, 'But we did not know this....' The *Quran* is never taught in simple Urdu or Hindi. It is read from one end to the other in Arabic, without any effort being made by the teacher to explain the meaning of the Ayats—the result being that the maulvis are given a free hand to interpret it.

Sometimes a case is highlighted and discussed when it comes into the limelight and society is awakened to the plight of the Muslim women. It happened in the case of Imrana, a mother of three, who had been raped by her father-in-law. She was told to marry her father-in-law and treat her husband and father of her children as her son. There were immediate reactions from the Muslim community. Educated, democratic, secular people say that these are tribal laws and tribal interpretations that have penetrated Islam. They even go to the extent of saying that Taliban is a tribal group and Islam is only being maligned because the West is against it. But then why doesn't any scholar of Deobandh/Bareli stand up and say that all this is un-Islamic.

All the so called Jehadi groups claim that they follow the Deobandi school of Islam. A friend, in an open letter, had requested the Deobandis to condemn the terrorists and distance the institution from these senseless killings and sectarian violence. The institution had refused to comment. Both of these major Muslim institutions have never said a word condemning the treatment of women, for the simple reason that women are not important enough, are not represented on decision making committees, and also because both men and the clergy have no problem with the way men treat women on the strength of religion.

Several *Jansunvais* and interviews later I decided to confirm the facts on my own and revisited the *Quran*; not just the original but also its translations, analysis and interpretations. I also read through the several Hadith compilations available and the Shariah. In the scriptures I made an important discovery. The rights and duties of women occur in a chapter that is also the chapter on property. This fact speaks volumes about how women were being treated in those times and the position that they enjoy in an Islamic society that claims to have forged itself on the basis of the Islamic scriptures.

Throughout the book I have given a number of examples from the *Quran* in an effort to prove that there is a vast difference between what the original scripture says and how it has been implemented. Several changes have been made to accommodate social norms, customs and traditions. Most scholars of Islam agree that Islam, as it is practised, is very different from what was advised in the *Quran*. In all the instances cited in this book, the *Quran* seems to have given a fairer deal to humanity in general, and women in particular, than what we actually see being executed. So is this book an exercise to show my support for the actual text, and do I recommend that it should be implemented?

In a discussion on laws for Muslim women, a participant had upheld the *Quran* and said that we should struggle to get what is written in it implemented in its totality. I did not agree. The *Quran* has relegated women to a secondary position, right from where it describes the formation of the universe and the creation of Adam and Eve. It accuses Eve as the cause of the original sin and the reason for Adam being thrown out of paradise; and to date women are being punished for this crime. Besides this accusation and several more of the same kind, the text leaves a number of gaps and room for loopholes—to dig out double meanings and to use the interpretation that suits their requirements and fulfills their particular need.

My contention is that no book of law can serve as the ultimate. Society has grown and developed and so has the need for change in laws to take care of the social, moral and statutory needs of the times.

After the death of the Prophet and with the spread of Arab power more and more conversions brought a huge population under the umbrella of Islam. Regional and personal beliefs infiltrated the practice of Islam and it was a requirement of the times that Islamic law and social pattern should be written down and be easily accessible so that everyone could follow Islam in its true essence. A couple of hundred years after the Prophet's death the process of coining and inscribing the Shariat began. Shariah means 'the right path'. In its accepted usage it refers to a path trodden by camels to the water source. Al-Shariat-al-Islamia, the complete name of what is generally referred to as just 'Shariah' means the Islamic way or right path to Islam. Shariat is based on the *Quran*, the Hadith and the life of the Prophet.

However, Shariah was optional and not completely binding on a Muslim till the Wahabi version of Islam surfaced.

Most of us living in a democratic set-up normally wake up to religious interference and inhuman cruelty when issues that were considered decided and sealed are opened up and treated in a diametrically opposite manner to the accepted human pattern. The case of Alicia Gali in May 2013 is one such incident. Alicia Gali, a citizen of Australia, was in the United Arab Emirates, working in a hotel. She was drugged and raped by three Muslim colleagues. When she regained consciousness, she went to hospital and reported the crime. But because the UAE follows Shariat law it favours Muslim men in rape incidents. Gali was charged with "sex outside of wedlock", found guilty and spent eight months in a UAE prison before her country and public outcry could secure her release and subsequent deportation.

These type of incidents would outrage most decent people. Anyone would think that a simple medical examination would prove the rape and the culprits would then be rounded up and charged as criminals. Secular progressive people find such occurrences especially frustrating because too often, religion provides immunity from prosecution or human rights abuse. It's one thing for an individual to use religion to justify his/her immoral, unethical or illegal opinions, but it enters a completely new level when the leaders of an entire community use the religio-legal system to pervert, elevate and advance the religious ideologies that serve as a mechanism to promote human rights abuses.

What about the double standards?

Substance and alcohol abuse is strictly prohibited in Islam and in the UAE. Before committing rape these men indulged in this crime. So they should have been rounded up for that. And what about sitting, drinking and talking to a woman who was not their wife, mother, sister or daughter? Again a sin, very conveniently overlooked.

Why do I narrate what has happened in other countries? Because most of these countries were moderate and liberal till recently. It is only in the near past that they have gone completely anti-women and barbaric. What is to stop these things beginning in India? On the sly? In interior regions? Before the police can act? Remember Roop Kunwar's murder, (termed Sati) and the support of the local population; remember the incident of Noorpur, Haryana. Mohini Giri was the Secretary of the Women's Commission for women. An adult Muslim girl who had married of her choice was abducted under the very eyes of Mohini Giri who had escorted the girl to the village to discuss a settlement and bring about a reconciliation….

Given the sudden emphasis on Muslim brotherhood and the insistence on uniformity of culture of Muslims—which was never an issue before, (Indian Muslims took great pride in being of Indian culture); formation of Pakistan and the formulation of Hudood laws that have since affected both Afghanistan and India, the training and coming up of Taliban in Pakistan as a counter force to Mujahideen who were comparatively liberal, the conquest of Taliban and their ruling Afghanistan for a few years, openly making a vulgar show of the violent, inhuman face of Islam—it is imperative that we must begin discussing laws. To protect the weak and create a more just and homogeneous society, Law must be a uniform umbrella that does not have leaks that drip religion, traditions, taboos and customs.

For too long people have been saying that the *Quran* is a perfect treatise, and it is the mullahs who are to blame for reinterpreting it in a manner so as to put the woman in a secondary position. This book is not an attempt to reinterpret the *Quran*, find inner, deeper meanings, or to prove that the original text gives equal rights to the woman. This is an attempt to show the contradictions within *Quran*, the way they have been highlighted and interpreted to give an edge to patriarchy, the manner in which tribal customs have been made out to be the actual Islam and the woman has been relegated to the position of being a non-entity.

This book is an effort to show that religious beliefs need to be segregated from law. No one has a problem with the Muslim way of worship, belief in the Prophet, Hajj, Ramzan, Namaz etc. But Muslims should have a problem with the way Islamic law is keeping half of the community away from the mainstream, deprived of what the Constitution guarantees, and which is a major hurdle in the development of the community.

Chapter - 1

Halala A Lawful Crime?

She was sitting curled up in a corner and had been quiet throughout. Zakia felt that she was desperate to say something. In a gathering of women it was impossible to maintain silence. All of them had something to say and wanted to say it at once. There was an audible hum of their constant chatter with sudden highs at which Zakia had to scold them like school children a couple of times.

"Please wait for your turn. Don't just begin speaking; raise your hand and wait for me to ask you to speak. How do you expect me to understand what you are saying if all of you speak together?"

Zakia would then look pointedly at her. She would smile and look away, usually downwards. Was there some awful shame that she was hiding? Zakia thought to herself.

Flanked by women on both sides, she was being nudged and poked to speak up. "Why don't you ask her? What was the point in coming all this way if you don't have the guts to speak?" They cajoled and persuaded, but she remained silent.

Three hours had passed. Zakia glanced pointedly at her wristwatch and began to collect her papers, pen and diary to indicate that the meeting to discuss the Shariat laws and the Indian Constitution was over. The women also got up and began to collect their security guards—a variety of hijabs, abayas, burqas—hanging from doors, hooks and nails, and began to wear them.

Zakia was moving towards the veranda where tea had been laid out when someone called from behind, *"Baji!"* Zakia swallowed her irritation and turned with a half-smile fixed on her face. This was a general occurrence; one or two of the audience would always maintain a silence throughout the meeting, and then when everybody began to disperse would expect a private discussion. Zakia knew that it could not be avoided since some women were reticent about speaking openly even in an all-woman gathering. It was understandable; after all, women had only just found their voices.

"*Baji*, I wanted to ask you something. You spoke for more than three hours on Shariat versus the Indian Constitution but you did not say a word about 'Halala'." She spoke all of this in a rush and then stuttered to a stop as if she had said something obscene that should not be mentioned amongst respectable people.

Zakia stopped and looked at her face for a full minute. How many times had she thought that this portion of the Surah-e-Nisa, the chapter on women and property in the *Quran*, should be discussed. But her work was to compare the Shariat laws and the provisions of the Indian Constitution, and try as she might, so far she had not been able to dig out an even remotely linked Act in the Constitution.

"What is your name?"

"Sakina."

"Tell me what do you wish to know about Halala."

She kept quiet. Zakia prodded her, "Your husband has divorced you?"

"Yes."

"And now he regrets it and wants to marry you again?"

"For the fifth time!" she mumbled.

Someone had placed a cup of tea in Zakia's hand. Shocked at Sakina's revelation, she almost dropped it. Taking a grip on herself, Zakia reached for her hand and moved to a corner. But she didn't have to ask any question to begin a dialogue. Sakina seemed to have been waiting for this privacy. Haltingly, stammering, the story of her life flowed out of her like a burst ulcer getting rid of rotting, foul smelling fluid.

"*Baji*, I was fourteen when the nikah with my husband Abdul Rashid was solemnised. My husband was eleven years older to me. He was fond of alcohol and was a frequent abuser of opium. Everyone, including my own parents, was aware of his addiction but then beggars cannot be choosers, and my parents, with five daughters, were literally beggars. On the whole, I was happy to be married. The family was well-to-do and there was only my brother-in-law, five years younger to me, besides my husband's parents. Everyone also believed that he would give up his bad habits once the wife was there to take care of things."

Sakina laughed in a strange manner, at herself and at the society that expected so much from a woman by way of correction and reformation, yet gave her practically no rights. She was expected to wage a war and win this battle without any weapons or arms.

She was quiet after her lonely laughter. Zakia tried to bring her back to the narration. "So when did the talaq happen?"

"The first time was six years after the marriage. I had two children by then. He came back one night dead drunk and demanded food. I put a small table near the place where he was sitting and put the plate of food before him. He was slouched on the chair and seeing the food tried straightening up and toppled the table. I was also tired after a full day of work and that was the last of the cooked food in the house. Irritably, I muttered, 'why do you drink so much that you have no control over your limbs?'

"That did it. He started shouting and abusing me, which he did in any case after getting drunk, and then he ended up by divorcing me in three pronouncements of talaq."

"But divorce given under intoxication is not valid."

"I did not know this and the maulvi did not give us the facts. Maybe he didn't know them either. I left for my parent's house. Thankfully, my children were so small and my mother-in-law so unwell that I was allowed to take my children with me. Anyway, when the intoxication wore off he wept and apologised, asked my pardon and went to maulvi sahib saying that he should solemnise the nikah again as he loved me a lot and could not live without me. Maulvi sahib told him that this was impossible—first a hundred days of iddat would have to pass, then I would have to be married to someone else, who would then divorce me; this would have to be followed by a hundred-day iddat again, and only then could I be married to Abdul Rasheed.

"How could my husband tolerate that I have sex with another man? He came to my parents' house and said to me, 'Wait a while Sakina. I shall find out a way.' A year-and-a-half passed in his trying to find a way. One day he came to me very happy and said, 'Sakina get dressed, I have found out a way. I shall have you married to my younger brother Tariq Rasheed. He has promised to divorce you after the first night and then I shall be able to marry you.'

"I was apprehensive. How was I to accept my brother-in-law, five years my junior, as my husband, even for one night? But my husband cajoled and persuaded and refuted each of my objections with one single counter argument: Who was I to object when maulvi sahib did not have any problem with this arrangement? After all, he was the caretaker of our religion. I also thought that when the maulvi had accepted then it must be admissible in the eyes of religion and Allah. I was married to my brother-in-law and late in the night he came to my room and bolted the door. I was sitting facing the wall, embarrassed even at the thought of showing my body to another man. When I did not feel him coming any closer for quite some time, I turned and saw him standing with folded hands, looking down at the ground like a sinner unable to meet the eyes of the world.

"Haltingly, I asked him, 'Is anything the matter?'

"He looked up and said, '*Bhabhi*, sleep on the bed. I'll lie down on the mat on the floor. I agreed to this arrangement because I wanted you back in this house. You are like my elder sister. I cannot even think of touching you. It is just for a night.'

"To tell you the truth *Baji*, that was the last time I had a dreamless, secure night. Next morning I was divorced again. Somehow, the hundred days of iddat passed and I was married to Abdul Rasheed again.

"But does a man ever change his ways? It is said that a piece of charcoal can be washed white but a man's character can never be changed. He had the same friend circle, the same habit of drinking and smoking opium. He would come back late, pick up a quarrel for no rhyme or reason and then begin beating me. In between, he would also keep abusing me, saying, 'You have stayed a night with my brother. He is sixteen years younger to me. I am growing old and he is full of youth and vigour. Did you enjoy it more with him? Do you miss him when you are with me? Do you go to him when you have the opportunity in the afternoons when I am not there and Ammi and the children are asleep?'

"*Baji* I tried to keep the secret for as long as I could. At last I could bear it no longer and it burst out from me. 'Why do you keep accusing poor me and your angel of a brother of having committed this sin? He did not even touch me that night. Even now he comes back home late because he does not wish to meet my eye.' He embraced and kissed me then, calling me his life and his beloved. I was grateful that he believed me, and there was peace in the house for a few months. Then, one evening, while he was drinking with friends, one of them teased him about having a wife whose ex-husband also lived under the same roof. How did he know that they were not making love behind his back? Abdul Rasheed was not able to tolerate this. 'My wife is only mine, understand? That nikah was just a sham. My brother did not even touch her,' he boasted. A declaration like this, made on a *theka*—how could it not spread? And having spread through the small township, how could it not reach the ears of maulvi sahib? And knowing the facts how could he not, as a protector of the true faith, take steps to show the world that he did not let the grass grow under his feet?

"My nikah to Abdul Rasheed was annulled and again for me began a period of iddat and the search for another man who would marry and divorce me, and in the process set me free to be married to my original husband. Of course, it could not be my brother-in-law this time, because he had been proved untrustworthy. How could anyone believe a man who did not force himself on his legally wedded wife and left her untouched?

"Another man was found and I was married to him. The next day this man flatly refused to divorce me. For fourteen long months I was his wife. I would happily have remained his wife forever but it was Abdul Rasheed who refused to adjust to the changed situation. He would see me in the market place buying vegetables or taking the children to school. He would recognise the burqa, come up to me and begin howling, literally. He would roll on the road, like a child throwing a tantrum. 'Oh Sakina, how can I live without you? Oh my life, come back to me.'

"In the end it was I who prevailed upon my husband to divorce me because I was being torn to bits, pulled from each side. I was the comic relief in the mundane life of the small town. People would inform each other that the entertainment had begun and converge to the spot. There would be laughter, catcalls that shamed me and earned Abdul Rasheed the nickname of 'Majnu'. So I was a divorcee again, counting the hundred days and waiting to be married to a man who said he loved me but could not stop himself from pronouncing talaq on the smallest pretext. The nikah was over, a few happy weeks passed and the same life surfaced again. It was as if he had become addicted to divorcing me. At the drop of a hat, without any proper reason, sometimes drunk, at others completely in his senses he began divorcing me. Then he would find another man, make all the preparations for the wedding and himself arrange for the maulvi. Once it was the maulvi himself who married me and ravaged me for six nights before giving a divorce. Periods of iddat would pass; I often lost count of the days, but Abdul Rasheed would be back exactly on the hundred and first day to marry me again. In this manner *Baji*, sixteen years of my life have passed spinning like a top between Nikah, Talaq, iddat and Halala.

"Oh *Baji!* Are those tears in your eyes? Strange! Or perhaps not so strange! Maybe this is how it should be. Strangers should take on the business of weeping at my plight because my own tear glands have long run dry...."

THE *QURAN* doesn't make any provision for a situation where multiple marriages and divorces can take place between the same man and woman. Did even Allah, the creator of the Universe, all living things and human beings, not realise that someone could be a repetitive sinner and use the law meant to be a 'deterrent' in his favour? Incidentally, there are different punishments prescribed for repetitive culprits of other crimes in the *Quran* but not for one who repeatedly divorces and marries the same woman.

Since the question of Halala arises only when the talaq has taken place it would be in order to discuss talaq or divorce in Islam first.

The followers of Islam take great pride in the fact that Islam is the first religion that accepts marriage to be a contract and thus negotiable, dissolvable and breakable. It introduced the idea of two people, legally married, deciding to live separately, taking other partners in a lawful manner. Other religions have borrowed the concept from Islam and introduced it in their law.

This is not entirely true. Divorce has existed in the tribal communities where the rights of the individuals are recognised and women and men enjoy a balanced position in society. Yet, it may be conceded that in an organised, monotheistic religion and a well-documented one, Islam is the first to allow individuals to dissolve a marriage.

Divorce in Islam can be initiated both by husband and the wife. When a man has initiated a divorce, the procedure is called talaq; when a woman does so, it is called khula. There are separate rules for divorce for men and women under the terms of Islamic law (Shariat). It is necessary to point out here that while talaq is easily obtained, getting khula is quite difficult.

The Muslim husband may initiate the divorce process by pronouncing the talaq, the formula of repudiation, three times. The first two times the talaq is pronounced, it may be withdrawn. But the third time it is pronounced, the divorce is irrevocable.

What does the *Quran* Say?

The Triple Talaq in one sitting is not mentioned in the *Quran*. According to the Holy Book, there is a waiting period involved between the three times a man can declare the divorce. This allows him to cool down, if he had started the talaq proceeding in anger or under duress of some kind. This gap is provided to resolve disputes, and also to be able to determine if a child is being born.

Differences within

Shia and Sunni Muslims have different rules for performing an Islamic divorce. Sunni practice requires no witnesses, and allows a husband to end a relationship by saying the one, two or triple talaq in a single breath.

Sunni scholars admit that this practice is wrong and against the Quran and the various Hadith, yet they allow it to continue and accept it as final. The Triple Talaq removes any opportunity or effort towards reconciliation with the help of mediators from each family. It also takes away the woman's right to give some explanation of her behaviour, conduct, act, which may have been cited as the reason for divorce.

Shia practice, on the other hand, requires two witnesses, followed by a waiting period. Mediation can bring about reconciliation and cohabitation in the period between the two pronouncements and result in the divorce being avoided. Shia scholars view the Triple Talaq in one sitting as a pagan pre-Islamic custom forbidden by Prophet Muhammad and, thus, sinful (*haraam*). It is believed that the Triple Talaq was reinstated by Umar ibn al-Khattab, the second Caliph. This revival of the pagan traditions is amongst the first of the reappearance of tribal practices, which became laws within Islam, that could not be contested.

In both the Sunni and Shia sects, a period of iddat (three months and ten days) follows the pronouncement of the talaq for the third time, after which the couple is divorced and the husband is no longer responsible for the wife's expenses, but remains responsible for the maintenance of the children, until they are weaned.

According to the *Quran*, the talaq involves three steps:

Initiation
Reconciliation
Completion
However, even here, there are differences between sects:

Initiation

While for most Sunni scholars initiation consists of the husband saying talaq once in the presence of his wife, most Shia scholars believe it must be a public announcement in the presence of at least two witnesses.

The *Quran* supports divorce as follows:

'O Prophet! When ye do divorce women, divorce them at their prescribed periods, and count (accurately), their prescribed periods: And fear Allah your Lord: and turn them not out of their houses, nor shall they (themselves) leave, except in case they are guilty of some open lewdness; those are limits set by Allah: and any who transgresses the limits of Allah, does verily wrong his (own) soul: thou knowest not if perchance Allah will bring about thereafter some new situation.'

—*Quran*, Sura 65 (At-Talaq), Ayat 1

Reconciliation

According to Sunni and Shia jurisprudence, the couple is supposed to try to reconcile during the waiting period, with the help of mediators from each family. If the couple breaks the waiting period by engaging in sexual intercourse, they are deemed to have been reconciled and the divorce is declared void.

'And if you fear a breach between the two, then appoint a judge from his people and a judge from her people; if they both desire agreement, Allah will effect harmony between them, surely Allah is Knowing, Aware.'

—*Quran*, Sura 4 (An-Nisa), Ayat 35

Completion

After the completion of the talaq procedure, the couple are divorced. The husband is no longer responsible for the wife's expenses. She becomes non-mahram (forbidden) for him and so they must observe the hijab (separation or veiled presence) rules.

Shia scholars say that when the waiting period (iddat) is over, two witnesses are required to witness the completion of the talaq, only then is the talaq complete and binding.

In support of this the *Quran* says:

'Thus when they fulfill their term appointed, either take them back on equitable terms or part with them on equitable terms; and take for witness two persons from among you, endued with justice, and establish the evidence (as) before Allah. Such is the admonition given to him who believes in Allah and the Last Day. And for those who fear Allah, He (ever) prepares a way out.'

—*Quran*, Sura 65 (At-Talaq), Ayat 2

The *Quran* also admonishes men saying:

'And when you divorce women and they reach their prescribed time, then either retain them in good fellowship or set them free with liberality, and do not retain them for injury, so that you exceed the limits, and whoever does this, he indeed is unjust to his own soul; and do not take Allah's communications for a mockery, and remember the favor of Allah upon you, and that which He has revealed to you of the Book and the Wisdom, admonishing you thereby; and be careful of (your duty to) Allah, and know that Allah is the Knower of all things.'

—*Quran*, Sura 2 (Al-Baqara), Ayat 231

Aftermath

If the wife is divorced for the third time, she becomes *haraam* (totally prohibited) for her former husband.

Even if divorce separates a man from his wife, he has to seek her help for bringing up the child, or of another female if the mother agrees. In such a case, the husband must pay for her expenses.

In Practice

In most Islamic states it is generally unacceptable for a divorced woman to live alone (as is usually also the case with unmarried women). In most situations women will return to live with their parents or to the household of another close relative.

'And when you have divorced women and they have ended their term (of waiting), then do not prevent them from remarrying when they agree among themselves in a lawful manner; with this is admonished he among you who believes in Allah and the last day, this is more profitable and purer for you; and Allah knows while you do not know.'

—*Quran*, Sura 2 (Al-Baqara), Ayat 232

'For divorced women maintenance should be provided on a reasonable scale. This is a duty on the righteous.'

—*Quran*, Sura 2 (Al-Baqara), Ayat 241

After divorce, the *Quran* specifies responsibilities on the divorcee and divorcer on behalf of their children. It also prohibits interventions from the previous husband in the divorced woman's life.

Talaq-i-Bid'ah means innovated (or sinful) form of divorce.

It is defined as a divorce which is pronounced thrice in one sitting when the wife is in the state of purity (*tuhr*), ie, when the man says: "I divorce you, I divorce you, I divorce you." The Hanafis (one of the four Sunni schools of fiqh/law jurisprudence named after scholar Abu Hanifa, b 699AD, Kufa, Iraq) believe that though this form of divorce is sinful and innovative, it is nevertheless valid and the divorce will take place. According to the Hanafis, when triple divorce is pronounced, the wife will become totally alienated from the husband and he cannot remarry her.

She becomes *haraam* for him. He can neither take her back nor go for a fresh nikah with her. He can go for nikah with her only after she marries another person and that person divorces her on account of marital conflict or she becomes a widow.

Maulana Umar Ahmad Usmani, a scholar from Karachi with liberal progressive views, stands against polygamy and Triple Talaq, which he discusses in detail in his eight-volume book *Fiqh al Quran*. According to him, this is the position of not only Abu Hanifa but also of Imam Malik (Malik ibn Anas, a highly respected scholar of Fiqh in Sunni Islam, b 711AD in Medina, Saudi Arabia), and Imam Shafi'i (a distant blood relative of the Prophet). A student of Imam Malik, Imam Shafi'i later took a stand different than his teacher in the interpretation of the fiqh saying this form of divorce is perfectly valid... "it is not innovation (*bid'ah*)... it is quite proper on the part of the husband to pronounce such a divorce. No husband can be prevented from adopting this as a valid course." Even Imam Ahmad Hanbal's (Sunni theologian, founder of the Hanbali school of jurisprudence, born in Baghdad, 780 AD) position is the same as that of Imam Hanifa and Imam Malik. Thus, it seems that all major founders of the four schools of jurisprudence accept the validity of triple divorce.

But, Imam Taymiyyah (Islamic scholar and philosopher of Turkey, 13th century, imprisoned for opposing the doctrine that would curtail the ease with which a Muslim man could divorce his wife) has proved that Imam Ahmad bin Hanbal had retracted from his earlier position of accepting the validity of triple divorce. He said that when he reflected on the Quranic position he came to the conclusion that it permitted only *raj'i talaq*, ie, divorce in which the wife could be taken back. He then took the position that even if someone pronounced triple divorce it should be treated as one only. The husband thus would have the right to take his wife back within the iddat period, or go for nikah if the iddat period had expired. Imam Ahmad's companions and disciples also adopted this position. Many companions of the Noble Prophet like Ibn Abbas (Caliph from 749-754, founder of the Abbassid dynasty which ruled over the eastern Islamic world for 500 years), Hazrat Ali (cousin and son-in-law of the Prophet and the first male to convert to Islam, Caliph from 656-661 AD), also were of this opinion. Some have quoted companions like Abdullah bin Mas'ud (companion of the Prophet and one of the early converts), Abdur Rahman bin'Auf (another companion of the Prophet, a trader by profession, a member of the committee that elected the first Caliph), and Zuber bin al-Awwam (one of the seven people to accept Islam, companion of the Prophet and a commander in the first army of Muslims) also adopting this position.

Ahl-e-Hadith (assembly of the followers of the 'sayings' of the Prophet) also are of this opinion—that triple divorce is not valid. The Ithna Asharis (the twelve Shias; the largest branch of Shia Islam) and Imamiyas (Shias believe in the twelve pious souls or Imams, descendents of the Prophet) believe that if three divorces are pronounced together, even one divorce does not take place, let alone three. Even some Hanafi jurists like Hajjaj bin Artat (contemporary of Muhammad ibn Muqatil) and Muhammad Ibn Muqatil (Hanafi scholar, supporter of the Abbasid Caliphate, appointed governor of the provincial capital Ifriqiya. He was very unpopular and had to be replaced due to the hatred of the people) believe that if one pronounces three divorces, no divorce will take place.

Maulana Usmani tells us that according to Muhammad Muqatil, one of the two opinions of Imam Hanifa was that only one divorce will take place if three divorces are pronounced. Similarly, according to Imam Tilmisani (a contemporary scholar of Imam Malik who took a stand against Triple Talaq), Imam

Malik also held the opinion that only one divorce takes place if three divorces are pronounced. Usmani also quotes from Hafiz Ibn Hajar's *Fath al-Bari* (famed scholar of Egypt of the 8th century AD. *Fath al-Bari* is his famous book that is a compilation and analysis of the Hadith) to the effect that many eminent jurists held that if one pronounces three divorces, only one takes place.

From among the Ulema of the later period, Sheikh Shaltut, also known as Sheikh al-Azhar (prominent Egyptian Sunni scholar who campaigned for dialogue between different sects of Islam), writes in his *Fatwa* that if one gives three divorces, only one divorce *Talaq-i-raj'i* will take place, and the husband will have the right to take his wife back by saying so or by having sexual contact with her. Another prominent 'Alim 'Allama Rashid Rida (b 1865 in Egypt, great supporter of technology and science who insisted that Shariah should be the law of the land of any Islamic State) in his *Tafsir al-Manar* (Vol IX p 683) has expressed a similar opinion. Another contemporary eminent Arab, 'Alim Shaikh Jamal al-Din al-Qasim (a scholar who has discussed Triple Talaq in great length and concluded that it has no validity) has discussed this problem at great length in his book *Al-Istinas* and concluded that triple divorce has no validity and it should be treated as one divorce only. Quoting all these authorities, Maulana Usmani says that triple divorce is not in keeping with the rulings of the *Quran*.

He then discusses the whole issue in the light of the Holy *Quran*. He refers to the Quranic verse 2: 229-30, which begins with *Al-talaqu marratan,* and explains that the word *marratan* implies a gap between two pronouncements, which means there should be a large enough time-gap between the two pronouncements of divorce. He says, "I went to your house twice but you were not there," cannot mean one went to someone's house twice in one go; it means there was some reasonable gap of time between the two visits. Thus, the act of going had to be accomplished in two different periods of time." Maulana Usmani then quotes other verses of the *Quran* where the word *marratan* occurs and explains that everywhere it implies a gap of time in between.

The question is—if despite triple divorce being sinful, innovative and against the *Quran*, would it occur if someone pronounced triple divorce? The second question is— did anyone make such a mistake (of pronouncing triple divorce) in the Prophet's time and did he accept it as triple divorce? Or did he take it to be one divorce only? Lastly, when did the practice of triple divorce start again?

In the *Quran*, nikah is described as *misaqan ghaliza*—a strong bond. It has explained how and with whom one can enter into this strong bond and this strong bond cannot be dissolved without proper reason and method. It certainly cannot be dissolved whimsically. According to the *Quran*, divorce is not an arbitrary and whimsical thing.

Maulana 'Usmani quotes from *Musnad Ahmad Ibn Hanbal* that once Rukanah pronounced three divorces against his wife but later he was very sorry for it. When the Prophet asked him, "How did you divorce your wife?" Rukanah replied that he had pronounced three divorces. The Prophet again queried, "Did you pronounce it in one sitting?" When he replied in the affirmative, the Prophet said, "Treat it as one divorce only and if you want you can take your wife back." And Rukanah took his wife back.

This Hadith of the Prophet narrated by Ibn Abbas is found in *Sahih Muslim, Sunan Abu Da'ud* and other authentic collections of Hadith literature. No one has questioned its authenticity pertaining to marriage, divorce, inheritance or custody of children. He bases his views entirely on the *Quran* and Hadith.

Maulana Usmani points out that Hazrat Umar had enforced triple divorce and it had become law. It was within the power of the caliph of the time to enforce certain ordinances in view of the prevailing situation, or to meet some crisis situation and no one could question it. It is, therefore, possible that Ibn Abbas might have given a *fatwa* accepting triple divorce after Hazrat Umar enforced the ordinance. The original Hadith, accepting three divorces as one, therefore, is not affected, maintains Umar Ahmad Usmani. Thus, it is proved by this Hadith that during the time of the Noble Prophet, triple divorce, if pronounced by someone, was accepted as one divorce only.

Then the Maulana takes up the third question-- when did the triple divorce begin to be accepted as three divorces? It is well-known that Hazrat Umar, after the initial two years of his *Khilafat*, had enforced triple divorce as final divorce and no one was permitted to take his wife back after pronouncing three divorces at one go. To substantiate his point the Maulana refers to the noted Egyptian historian Muhammad Husain Haykal's book *Umar al-Farouq* in which the author says that Umar made such an *ijtihad* (interpretation) in what is well established Quranic injunction in 2: 229-30. Until today, we are opposing Hazrat Umar in this matter because the *Quran* requires all attempts for reconciliation before a divorce.

So if the *Quran* was being followed, as Muslims are instructed to do, a case like Sakina's would never have happened. Persuasion, reconciliation or intervention of family and friends was not a possibility. She herself says that her husband regretted his pronouncement of 'triple talaq' almost immediately—that he apologised and wanted to make amends. He admitted that he had spoken the words in a fit of anger or in an intoxicated state. Yet, it was binding on him, who was actually the guilty one and on her who was innocent.

Repercussion or punishment in the other world on disobeying Allah's word generates fear. Should a man and woman continue to cohabit after the triple talaq it would be considered adultery.

Burning in hell is a frightening proposition for the believer.

More than what would happen in the after world is the social stigma and alienation in this life. A divorced woman is looked down upon and so is one who lives outside a religio-legal arrangement. So most women accept 'triple talaq' as a finality so that they can move on.

Maybe there is someone out there, or a whole group of people out there who are getting some kind of pleasure in forcing women into a life of indignity and unhappiness.

Chapter - 2

Stage-managed Halalas

Holding a placard, 'Halala is nothing but the vilest of rapes', the frail and waif-like Rubaiya Ahmed stands in the centre of a group of forty-odd women protesting the draconian laws for women in Islam at the Hazrat Mahal Park in Lucknow.

The venue chosen assumes significance as the park is named after Hazrat Mahal, one of the consorts of Nawab Wajid Ali Shah, the last ruler of Awadh, who struggled for power, dignity and prestige and opted for a life of exile instead of one of indignity. Hazrat Mahal had been a washerwoman—a woman from the working class, who had been seen washing clothes on the bank of the river by the last Nawab as he drove his open *bugghi* accompanied by three other wives. She was not very beautiful and was not fair. But she had a well-sculpted body, taut bustline and on the whole a sensuous figure. This had been acquired through the continuous pounding of clothes on the slabs of stones set in a line on the *dhobi ghat.* The Nawab had got down to speak to her and she had talked to him with the confidence of a woman who knows that she does not depend on anyone for her needs; that she feeds herself and those dependent on her with honest work.

He is said to have gone back to his palace, divorced one of the wives he was now tired of, since Islam allowed only four wives at a time; and with the blessings of Allah—for Nawab Sahib was a God fearing Muslim—married the washerwoman, and named her Hazrat Mahal.

When the East India Company and its Governor, Lord Cornwallis, decided to annex Awadh, Nawab Wajid Ali Shah abdicated without a fight and agreed to migrate to Kolkata (then Calcutta). It was then that Begum Hazrat Mahal decided to fight and proved that the land belonged to those who worked it with the sweat of their brow.

She took charge of the affairs, seized control of Lucknow, and set up her son, Prince Birjis Qadir, as the Wali-ahad (crown prince) of Awadh. The British were not going to give up just because a new ruler had been placed on the throne and a woman was conducting the day-to-day functioning of the state even though Great Britain was being ruled by a woman—the 'powerful and just' Queen Victoria. Prince Birjis Qadir was soon forced to abandon his throne. Hazrat Mahal built up an army, rejecting the promises of allowance and status held out to her by the British. She fought the British, winning initially but then losing and retreating, till she was driven to the Tarai region. From here she sent a plea for asylum to the King of Nepal, who though a staunch Hindu, accepted her claim to the throne of Awadh. She migrated to Nepal, where her son Birjis Qadir was given a high rank in the army of Nepal. She died in 1879.

Nawab Wajid Ali Shah divorced Hazrat Mahal much before he moved to Kolkata. It is not known if he had become tired of her rustic, working class beauty. Or did he find her too independent, too straightforward, too unyielding to the hypocritical ways of the Awadh court and the royal household?

Rubaiya Ahmed is sixty-three years old. Socially speaking she should be praying most of the time to improve her lot in the afterlife. Many would expect her to be preparing for Hajj, turning her back on material possessions, passing her delectable recipes as family heirlooms to her daughters-in-law, and taxing her memory for bedtime stories for her grandchildren. She should certainly not be standing in the relentlessly beating sun, protesting about something that women are too ashamed to even discuss among themselves, holding a placard that seems too heavy for her thin arms, shouting slogans that nobody cares to hear or register.

"Yes, thirty-eight years have passed. But does the brain have the capacity to erase what has been etched on one's soul?" She shudders as she recalls the darkest night in the sixty-three years of her life. Women around listen to her in silence. They have all been forced to go through this and all of them have come out of it mutilated and deformed. "It was as if my soul had been ripped from my body and dragged over a thorny babool bush. The thorns not just piercing and hurting but giving wounds that would begin to bleed at the mere remembrance of the incident. Curses would flow, for my fate, for my husband, for my female form and for my children!"

"Children, why children? The poor dears!"

"Well it was for them that I agreed to the humiliation—when I allowed another man into my bed. I did not, could not, give up my children. The youngest one was a little more than six years old, and once divorced, I would have no right on them. I would have to go away to my parent's house, live out my life alone or wait for some angel to descend and marry me. I would not even have the money and resources to travel from my village to Lucknow to meet my children on festivals. How could I just forget them? And they would surely have forgotten me. How could I let myself become a stranger to my children?"

Could a system of law be so unjust? Could it deny the natural bond between the mother and the child?

Triple Talaq was pronounced in one go, in a fit of anger, on a trivial altercation. There were witnesses around, so no hiding it, and since talaq has a conclusiveness about it, there was no going back. After sleeping over the incident, the husband's anger had dissipated. He had requested, even begged the witnesses to forget the previous night. But it was already too late. Word had reached the local maulvi and he had arrived with the Holy *Quran* asking the witnesses to swear with their hand on the Holy Book that the talaq had not been pronounced. Naturally, no one was willing to do so, and the talaq formally came into existence with the period of iddat beginning from the same day.

"My husband's sister came to see me a week after that. My children were crying for me; there was no one to look after them. My husband was missing me and wanted me back and so a Halala had been fixed.

"How could I do it? How could I sleep with a man for a single night? And what about my husband? How would he accept me back as his life partner, as his wife?— A woman who had gone to another man for a night. How was I then different from a prostitute? She would spend a night with a man to earn some money, I would be doing the same to earn a family.

"I said all this and my sister-in-law argued back, contesting every point, persuading me to come back and take care of what was mine and to accept this path since it was the only one open to me.

"Then I asked that last, perhaps the most important question. 'Who was this who was willing to do this for me and my family? Who was this man I should be treating as an angel but I could only think of as a fiend, as a usurper, as a luster?'

"My sister-in-law looked the other way, then down at her feet, then held my hand and said, 'I do not mind'."

"You mean...."

"It is my husband. He would be good to you. And then it is just for one night."

One night! Is there a difference in being raped and defiled once or several times? Rape remains rape.

"Please agree, *Bhabhi*. Accept this one punishment for a life of bliss."

"She was right. Punishment it was; but for what crime? I had not committed one. If anyone was at fault it was my husband. He was the one who should have been taken to task for losing his temper; punished for going to the extent of even thinking of talaq, and publicly humiliated for putting his lawfully wedded wife through this mental agony and torture. Instead, he was to go scot-free and I was to be punished. I bore the humiliation of being a divorcee, the pain of separation from my children, the indignity of allowing an unknown man into my bed. I accepted his roving, grabbing, fondling, probing hands, quelling the revulsion that rose in each cell of my body. How many times would he rape me through the night? I would live every moment of that single night marriage with the tension of whether he would or not pronounce talaq the next day. Would he or would he not set me free? His wife, my sister-in-law had agreed to his second marriage. What was to stop him from not divorcing me for as long as he liked?

"Oh! the shame of it. Living just four houses away from this husband of a night and then back to being brother-in-law and sister-in-law. He would visit, come for festivals, family gatherings, funerals. His eyes would travel all over my body and I would know he was mentally undressing me. Not just me, everyone would know. They would exchange knowing glances; womenfolk would in family quarrels throw this at my face. 'You are a Halala.' Others would joke and ask me which man had been a better performer. How many things can I tell you? I have lost count of how many times I have wished myself dead.

"I am here because I do not want this to happen to any other woman. I want the law to be changed; I demand a life of dignity!"

Rubaiya belonged to the middle class. She was a graduate and had been working in a village school before being married. Once married, she had given up her job but not given up reading. From newspapers and magazines to serious novels and poetry—she dedicated at least four to five hours to keeping herself informed of national and international politics and social debates. In her late fifties, she had taken a short course of applied computers and was now an asset to the organisation that took up cases related to *Muslim Personal Law*, handling the correspondence, counselling the victims and compiling the monthly newsletter.

Talking about the purity of the woman that patriarchy upholds with all its strength, Rubaiya asks, "If the Halala and talaq are lawfully conducted, does it mean an end to a woman's indignity? What after that? For my husband I had been so negligible an entity that he could divorce me over a petty quarrel (something that happens all the time between every husband and wife), get me married to another man, and get him to divorce me. Would he marry me again after the period of iddat? Suppose he was to change his mind—suppose he could not come to terms with an impure woman who had been defiled by another man. Where would I be then? Divorced by one man, defiled by another, living alone, having lost my children. What would I be? Like this Shaista here!"

THE *QURAN* expounds: 'So if a husband divorces his wife (for a third time), he cannot after that remarry her until after she has married another husband and he has divorced her. In that case, there is no blame on either of them if they reunite, provided they can keep the limits ordained by Allah. Such are the limits ordained by Allah which He makes plain to those who know.' (2:230)

The Muslim husband may initiate the divorce process by pronouncing the talaq, the formula of repudiation, three times. The first two times the talaq is pronounced, it may be withdrawn. But the third time it is pronounced, the divorce is irrevocable. A man has to pronounce talaq first time, wait for a period of one month, repeat it again for the second time, wait again for a month and then repeat it the third time. After the third time, a period of 'iddat' of three months and thirteen days has to be observed by the wife and she is not to marry any other man in this period. Reconciliation is possible in the gaps between the pronouncement of the first two talaqs and even in the period of iddat. If this happens the talaq is void. However, if the period of iddat is over and no reconciliation has taken place, divorce becomes a finality.

After pronouncing talaq, the wife becomes *haraam* for the husband. If he wants to remarry the same woman, the rules are set. Once the mandatory iddat period gets over, the woman has to get married to someone else. This marriage has to be consummated. After the second husband divorces the woman, the first husband is free to marry her once again after another iddat period.

However, Halala-fixing is strictly prohibited in Islam. It can also not be planned in advance.

The nikah between the woman and the second husband, with an understanding of a divorce afterwards, will not be valid, if this is planned. It will be an illegitimate relationship with the second husband, and with the first husband also, with whom she comes to live after a pre-planned Halala.

Prophet Muhammad has cursed both such men—those who perform Halala and for whom Halala is performed. The second

Caliph, Hazrat Umar, ruled during his reign that he would punish with stoning to death those who performed a pre-planned Halala. Imam Sufian Sauri says: "If someone marries a woman to make her halal (for her ex-husband) and then wants to keep her as wife, he is not permitted to do so unless he solemnises a nikah afresh, as the previous nikah, conducted as a plan, shall be considered unlawful."

In reality this is what actually happens:

A man divorces his wife in a fit of rage someday. After sometime his anger cools down, and coming to his senses he realises his mistake. The man wants to take the woman back in his life, but the maulvi of his town tells him that the only option for this is Halala—which then can make her, the ex-wife, lawful for him. He explains to the man that to remarry his wife, first he would have to allow her to get married to another man who would consummate the marriage as her lawful husband. If the man divorced her, then and only then, could he remarry her after she had spent the iddat period.

Actually, Halala is not a means of remarrying a wife after uttering divorce. When a man permanently divorces his wife by uttering three talaqs he cannot remarry her at any cost. Only if the woman decides to have a second marriage to spend the rest of her life peacefully and for the sake of the future of her children (if any), and at any point of time, if the second husband also divorces her of his own accord, as a matter of coincidence, or if he dies, and if the woman also wants to get back to her first husband, she can remarry her first husband. This process would be called Halala. This brings in so many coincidences that it becomes an impossibility. It is an open challenge to the creativity of the man's mind to find novel ways and means to assuage his perverted desires. He gets plenty of opportunities to play God.

So, the whole process is based on a number of coincidences and on the willingness of the woman to get back. Halala is not an option to get her back by stage-managing a temporary marriage where everything is planned or agreed upon. For a sum of money a man can be found who agrees to marry the divorced woman, only to divorce her after having physical relationship with her for a stipulated or mutually agreed period of time. Normally this period is one day to one week. He then divorces her according to the agreement in order to make her lawful for her first husband.

And this has become a widely accepted practice across Muslim societies. In many towns, the maulvis (priests) arrange for a man for the marriage of such a divorced woman by paying him a specific fee. This man marries and divorces the woman after consummating the marriage. In most of the cases all the expenses of the marriage and the fee are paid by the former husband.

In recent years, the practice of administering Halala has taken an ugly turn as corruption has crept into the clergy and in the society at large—in the religious affairs that have become both a means of earning money, and getting the opportunity to legally keep a mistress for a short period of time, without having to worry about any social or legal hassles.

In recent reports from Europe, in many towns and cities with Muslim population the muftis themselves have taken up the lofty task of serving the Muslim Ummah by offering their services of Halala, by marrying such hapless women to make them lawful for their former husbands. According to reports, one mufti has even established a 'Halala centre' to cater to the needs of such bad-tempered husbands, as well as the filthy rich with uncontrollable lust who want to keep concubines for short periods of time.

According to the editor of Newageislam.com, Sultan Shahin, such Halala services are also offered by the managing committee members of some mosques in western countries (in Brussels, Belgium for example) where the managing committee consists of rich people who are ready to offer Halala services. The richest of them gets to perform Halala with the most beautiful woman who comes for this purpose. A *fatwa* of divorce is given most easily, sometimes on the flimsiest grounds, and sometimes without any grounds whatsoever. This is accepted by the husband's family largely as the *fatwa* and offer of Halala is also accompanied by a threat of ex-communication by the priests.

The *Quran* and Hadith, both prohibit such a marriage and 'accursed are all those who are involved in such marriages'. Such a practice of Halala is *haraam* as it is in clear contravention of both the Hadith and the Quranic ordainments.

The custom of Halala has itself become a problem because of its misinterpretation and misapplication. Halalas or arranged marriages are paid-for-affairs in order to fulfill the minimum criteria to reunite with the spouse.

The Prophet has strictly prohibited such practices in the name of Halala and admonished those who misinterpret the verses of the *Quran*, to serve their own petty interests. According to a Hadith, the Prophet said:

'The Curse of Allah be upon the one who marries a divorced woman with the intention of making her lawful for her former husband, and upon the one for whom she is made lawful!' The Prophet cursed both the men who make the wronged woman go through humiliation and severe mental and psychological torture and cause her a permanent stigma. Clearly, the Prophet does not blame her, and absolves her of all responsibility in the entire episode, because he too believes that grave injustice has been meted out to the woman.

The Prophet curses the men but not the woman who must

have been persuaded or threatened to the point of accepting this arrangement. In a way, the Prophet accepts that the woman, though agreeing to the arrangement, is doing so because she has no other option; she is an unwilling party because of her helpless state. So she is absolved from the curse.

However, the manner in which 'arranged Halalas' are stage managed, it is the woman who is the victim and the woman who is punished.

Chapter - 3

Khula An Uplhill Task

Humera was sick of this life. It was as if she was continuously tightrope walking; balancing herself like a skilled acrobat so that she would not fall down. Every time she did something that displeased her husband he pronounced 'talaq' once. The next month would pass with her praying that the second pronouncement would not come. The month would pass and if he did not repeat it she would heave a sigh of relief and begin praying that he would not utter it again. The third time, he was so angry that he kept count of the days and right on dot repeated the 'talaq'. How she had prayed that the third pronouncement would not come and the talaq would not materialise.

Slowly, without her realising it, the joy of living receded from her being. She now existed from one day to another, acting to appear pleasant. Each day was spent in managing all her duties and housework as efficiently as she could, even during her spare time. She made notes to remember what had displeased her husband so as not to repeat the mistakes, debating and then outwitting herself into wiping out all her personal desires ranging from wishing to eat her favourite 'chaat' to going to the doctor for a bad attack of influenza, foregoing both necessities and needs as trivialities. Realisation hit her when the neighbourhood had suddenly erupted with 'the moon has been sighted, Eid Mubarak, Eid Mubarak' and she had shrugged and said 'so what!' She had looked at herself in surprise: what was wrong? Why did she have no enthusiasm for the festival? Why was she not rushing up the stairs to the roof to see the moon, close her eyes and open them only when she would see the face of a loved one? Her life of nine years rolled out before her as if in a film, and she saw herself transforming from a bright, fun loving, enthusiastic girl into a jittery, nervous woman, who committed blunders because she was so afraid of making mistakes.

Humera's mother-in-law was kind and often admonished her son Obaid for using the weapon of divorce. She loved Humera and took care of the two grandchildren during the day. Her father-in-law was an educated man and taught Chemistry in the nearby Government Senior Secondary School. It was he who had insisted on Humera completing her Masters in Social Work and taking up a job in an NGO. A loner by nature, Humera's father-in-law had of late begun taking Obaid with him during his long evening walks. It was Obaid who had revealed to her that his father discussed with him what the *Quran* said about short-tempered men who pronounced talaq in a fit of anger and advised him about curbing his temper as it was un-Islamic. Humera had been so grateful to her parents-in-law. She tried harder to please her husband, offered to give up her job (that she loved) if that was an issue, even tried to find out in discreet ways if his interest lay somewhere else, and if the cause for his random utterances of talaq was another woman. She drew a blank everywhere. He earned well; the house belonged to them, the children attended good schools. Yet, at the drop of a hat, Obaid would utter the first 'talaq' and her life would turn upside down for the next month. She could not refuse to accept talaq if it came. That was not an option provided by the Holy *Quran*. If a man pronounced talaq the woman just had to accept it; she had no right to question or ask the reason for the divorce. But a man could, amongst the Shia community of Muslims, say talaq the first two times, as many times as he wished.

It took her nine years to realise that she could not go on like this. She would have a nervous breakdown, or worse, commit suicide. She just had to bring to an end this uncertain, inconsistent existence. Did she or did she not belong? How long could one be expected to live in an unpredictable and unreliable relationship? She knew it would be a letdown for her in-laws, who were trying their best to make the marriage work. But she just couldn't go on. It had taken her a year to come to the decision. She was going to ask for 'khula'—calmly, without anger or emotions.

Anger and emotions, outbursts and humiliation had come later, when she had learnt how difficult it was to make a khula happen.

Humera was asked to give reasons for wanting khula. She was questioned if she had discussed this with her husband. Was he willing to give her khula? What was the amount of compensation that had been fixed and who were the inter-mediators? How could it be assured that the mediators did not have a vested interest? What did she plan to do after she got the khula? What was going to happen to the children? And the questioning and counter-questioning went on and on. Her reason, that she did not wish to live a life where the 'divorce' hung like a constant sword over her head, was taken as un-Islamic, since that was a man's right. She was also told that she should be grateful that she belonged to a sect that did not allow 'triple talaq', and consider herself fortunate that things never came to a head and her husband did not pronounce the third and final talaq—meaning that he loved her and so she must feel remorseful for even having thought of khula.

The advice and *fatwas* carried on as her demand was tossed back and forth between her and the *Muslim Personal Law Board*

'KHUL' IS an Arabic term that literally means 'to take out' or 'remove'.

Khula is the right of women in Islam to give divorce or get separated from their husbands. After divorce the husband is responsible for the education and maintenance of the children. The children live with the mother for seven years. After seven years the children have the right to live with the father or mother, as the parents decide.

Khula is basically an understanding or agreement that is reached between a husband and wife. The husband agrees to pronounce the talaq usually after a financial settlement. In the normal course it should simply be the dower or meher if it has been paid at the time of nikah. If it has not, then the meher is waived as compensation for being set free.

The Hadith gives an incident supporting this:

In the time of the Prophet, the wife of Thabit-ibne-Qais came to the Prophet and asked him to intervene on her behalf to obtain khula. The Prophet inquired about the terms and conditions of the nikah. He was told that an orchard had been given to her as the dower or meher at the time of marriage.

The Prophet then asked her if she was willing to give back to her husband the orchard he had given her. The woman accepted this demand and got khula.

The present scenario is that there are a large number of men who adopt a revengeful attitude of deliberately torturing women who do not wish to continue the alliance.

A majority of men are not willing to accept the fact that a woman is walking out of the marriage. So they put across some other demands. These demands are usually either a big sum of money or forfeiting her visiting rights to meet her children. In either case the woman is in a weak position. In the first case she might not have enough money to 'buy' khula. It may be that she wishes to live off the income of the land, house, orchard that the man is now demanding. Parting with these would reduce her financial and social status. In the second case, it simply amounts to emotional blackmail because no woman would want a divorce at the cost of cutting off all ties with her children.

Once the husband accepts the terms being offered and agrees to khula, he is asked to pronounce talaq in exchange.

Thus, it is up to the woman to somehow cajole, persuade and prevail upon the husband to give her a divorce. She has to waive her dower or part with a substantial amount of money, or sell off or gift immovable property to somehow bring the man to the point where he agrees to the parting of ways. Even after all this it is still the man who is divorcing the woman and not the woman divorcing the man.

The very concept of divorce is based on incompatibility. If the man does not want a woman, he has the right to leave her. Why doesn't she have the same right? Why is she compelled to give socially accepted reasons, and in modern times enforce an anti-dowry case, file police complaints or resort to lawlessness by hiring goons to terminate the marriage?

Supposing the man is adamant not to pronounce talaq and insists on a compensation that he knows the woman is unable to pay; on the other hand the woman is equally insistent upon obtaining khula—what happens then?

The Hadith tells us that in such a case a person respected in society and acceptable to both as mediator should be appointed by mutual consent. This person is to hear both sides, take stock of the financial status of both the parties, arrive at an amount to be paid as compensation to the husband and inform them of his decision. This decision would then be binding on both and khula would become a certainty.

In case of this arbitration, and if the woman refers her case to the *Muslim Personal Law Board* or to the maulvi nearby, she is immediately expected to provide reasons for her desire to separate from her husband. The maulvi consults the higher authority on behalf of the woman. The higher authority depends on the sect to which both belong as there are different schools with their specific interpretations of the *Quran* for every sect.

According to the Hadith, a woman does not need to give a reason for wanting khula. An incident quoted in the Hadith supports this.

A lady, married for six years, came to the Prophet and asked him to intervene as she wished to obtain khula from her husband. The Prophet inquired the reason for her wishing to dissolve the marriage. The woman kept silent. The Prophet again queried if her husband's character was questionable to which she answered that there was nothing wrong with his character as he was pious and God fearing. He then asked if he was hot tempered or physically abusive. The woman again replied in the negative. However, she was firm on her demand for khula. The Prophet then did not insist that she reveal the reason and awarded khula to her.

The Prophet is later said to have explained to his followers that, "If a man divorces he must present the reason to the Qazi; however if a woman wants a khula and she is not willing to reveal the reason, the Qazi must not insist and should award her the khula."

Here the Prophet takes into account that the Qazi would be a man and the woman would feel awkward in revealing personal or intimate experiences that may have led her to demand khula. It also allows for a woman to seek a divorce from one man because she prefers another and not reveal this fact to anyone. The decision of the Prophet also accepts that a woman must have examined all options, perhaps also requested the elders in the family to intervene and advise both, failing which she had to request for khula.

But contemporary *Muslim Personal Law* absolves the man from providing any reason for divorce, yet insists that the woman give a reason that is 'acceptable' to the Qazi.

There are innumerable incidents in history which reveal that the women got justice equal to men.

It is true that the woman (in the *Quran*) does have the right to terminate the nikah, but this can happen only under certain conditions and all these conditions are subject to the husband's consent. Unless he signs to give his consent, the khula is not considered valid. In the Indian *Muslim Personal Law*, there are forty-two clauses in favour of talaq and only four in favour of khula. Ironically, all the four clauses carry the condition of the husband's consent for the khula.

Contrary to the manner in which the Prophet acted and the explanation he gave to his followers, the contemporary *Muslim Personal law*s constituted by different communities provide the man every convenience to divorce the woman. As a result, the status of the woman has been totally marginalised. Her very existence in a relationship depends upon the whims of the man. He can divorce her even if he is drunk, in anger, if he is mentally unstable or even jokingly. But she is not given such a right. The man is free and can have a second or third marriage if he wants and there are no restrictions upon him from the law. She is compelled to wander around to prove she has been wronged, cheated, deprived, abused, tortured etc.

And of course, a reason such as Humera's, is no reason at all.

Chapter - 4

Sinners Go Scot-free

Rubaiya is angry. It is understandable. She has been subjected to the humiliation of Halala. She also meets new cases every day—women who have been through indignities of worse sorts in the course of Halala.

"It is the man who commits the crime of adultery or talaq. Instead of being apologetic and accepting his guilt before God and his wife, he hurriedly and without any deliberation takes the extreme and final step of Triple Talaq. If at all anyone has to be punished it should be the man. Beat him, flog him, jail him or make him do social service. But no! He is completely absolved of his crime by just the fact that he is now regretting his mistake, wishes to make amends and marry the woman again! It is good of Islam to be so generous and forgiving to the man. But then, in its forgiving, generous disposition, it does not stop there. It goes on to punish the woman! Why may we ask? What crime has she committed?"

As if the humiliation of being divorced in a fit of temper, with her meher thrown on her face, her children of seven years and above taken away from her was not enough, the upbraiding continues. It is the woman who has to go through the period of iddat; again it is she who has to be married to someone else; someone who in the first instance has agreed to marry and sleep with her only to divorce her.

"I felt totally numb and dead inside. But that was the only option left to reclaim my two sons," says Masooma. "Moreover, maulvi sahib had warned me that no one would participate in my funeral procession and my family would be ostracised if I flouted the Shariah's command."

Jalal, Masooma's 'husband' for one night, was not particularly bothered about her turmoil. He was there for a purpose—to help his cousin salvage his marriage. A night after the nikah and the mandatory consummation, he divorced Masooma without a fuss. For all practical purposes Masooma should have been grateful to Jalal, who did this without charging any 'fee'. He could not see the anguish of his cousin, who had divorced his wife in anger and wanted her back. After all blood is thicker than water and who else would help if not ones own relatives?

It has been seven years since Masooma got back with her first husband, but the horror of Halala has stayed on. "I feel as if the man I married died the day someone else defiled my body," she declares with vehemence. Her sons, then eight or nine, are now teenagers, and her only concern is to ensure somehow that they never get to know about the humiliation their mother faced, for "it would shatter them, or worse, they may blame me for the episode."

Can Masooma take any steps to see what happened to her does not happen to the girls her sons marry? She can teach them to respect women. She can also tell them that one should not pronounce talaq in a hurry and that it should be a well thought out decision. They began reading the *Quran* from the age of seven and there is no way that she can contradict what the maulvi is teaching them. "I cannot tell them that Halala is an injustice to women and Allah has not taken the woman's emotions and feelings into account while coining these Ayats. And that, however well drafted a legal system may be, it just cannot cover the whole range of the possibilities that the human mind can come up with; the distortions that can be invented, the loopholes found, the perversions masterminded and the mangled meaning misrepresented.

Rubaiya pulls a girl of about twenty-eight from the group. Ordinary looking, not educated, she has chapped fingers and cracked nails. Her name is Shaista. Her dress, caloused hands of a menial worker and body language proclaim that she probably works as a housemaid—the daily help who tries to work in as many houses as she can in a single day.

Rubaiya and Shaista belong to two different strata of society but are not very different in their fates. Rubaiya is educated, can work as an office assistant, proofreader, or accountant. The education she has received at her parent's house can now be used as a launching pad to further her skills and add new ones. In short, she can improve her earning capacity and manage a middle class existence.

Shaista, on the other hand, is almost illiterate, having skimmed through the Holy *Quran* with the help of the local maulvi, just once, to fulfill the demands of her would be in-laws. She doesn't recall having understood any of it and even if she did, it was quickly forgotten. She works in five houses. Two of them are Muslim households and three are Hindus. She is fortunate; all the ladies she works for are good women. They are generous with clothes for her and her children. One is a doctor, and Shaista has never paid for medicines since she has started working for her. All these educated, aware, liberal women want to help her. But they are helpless before the rigid, watertight laws of Islam as it is practied and accepted.

How could the fate of these two women, Rubaiya and Shaista, be the same when they are socially, economically and intellectually so different? Social reformers and activists have proclaimed that educated, economically independent women are important for development and change. The demand that women be allowed to educate themselves and become financially self-reliant, has in its background, the belief that women who are educated, would be able to rewrite their destinies. But can they? Can different, new fates be inscribed on an old, overwritten slate? Can old languages speak with a new vocabulary? Can old laws widen their parameters to make space for the new entrant—the educated woman?

The house help faces the usual problems of the 'have nots'. She has to work to eat and to feed others.

Shaista, who works from 7am to 7pm, wakes up at 4am to cook for the family, smiles as her mistress, indulges her pampered children, dreams of her children doing better than her in life, but is not quite sure what that 'better' is and how it is to be achieved. She is not ashamed of being a working woman. With three children, she did not expect her man Amjad to be the sole provider for the house.

Amjad was a scrap collector for a rich *kabari*, doing the rounds of the city and earning a rupee from every kilogram of old newspaper *raddi*. Shaista had begun working while unmarried. It was her savings that paid for her wedding. By contemporary definitions in social gradation, she should be considered economically independent. She paid for her food, clothes (usually hand-me-downs from the people she worked for), and she even paid for her own wedding! How much more independent can one get?

Shaista doesn't quite remember when she had begun accompanying her mother on her rounds as the daily partime help. She does remember that she would sweep the house before her mother mopped it and was scolded by the mistress for leaving dust in the corners and under the sofa. And she also remembers the sweets and other titbits handed to her in some houses.

She was about twelve when one of the mistresses had a baby and asked her mother to let Shaista stay for the day. Those were three good years. A good lunch, and snacks and tea twice a day; work was light and the baby was pretty, clean and smelt good. They allowed her to watch television while the baby slept and never scolded her. Every evening, when her mother came to pick her up it was with a bit of regret that Shaista left the cool, well-furnished house for the slums where they lived.

But the best was yet to come. It was the mistress of the house who suggested that a bank account be opened in Shaista's name and a portion of her salary saved. There had been a terrible quarrel at home. Her father saw no reason for this, and when her mother had pointed out that the savings would be useful for Shaista's marriage, he had argued that Allah would take care of everything. This is a statement never to be contested—any argument to this is immediately labelled '*kufr*' or blasphemy instigated by the devil. But Shaista's mother, like so many women in her situation, opted for blasphemy, perhaps because it came with reason and logic. She requested the mistress to open the savings account and keep the passbook in her possession.

Three years later, there was a mind boggling amount, or so it seemed, till the wedding date was fixed. The bridegroom's family had made all sorts of demands, knowing that there was a sumptuous kitty tucked away. Shaista had herself wanted quite a few things for herself and her new home. The savings were gone before she landed in her husband's house. But who cared? She was married and she was willing to continue to work. She was happy with her husband—the three children coming in quick succession added to her fulfillment.

Everything was working well until the fire at the scrap storage and sorting area.

How had things happened so fast? One day life was a slow, lazy rivulet, and the next it became a surging, gushing, mad, flooded, enraged, uncontrollable river—biting its banks and chewing up the bits of mud and flora like an insatiable demon.

Her husband lost the job because the courts ordered a ban on bulk storage of plastic, polythene and other inflammables within the urban residential areas. The owner was quick to appeal about the loss of his livelihood and the same court decried that he could now build a multi-storey complex on the land. The chance of getting back the job in future became bleak. Shaista did not have a problem with this. Allah often put to test his honest followers and one should bear these problems with a smile, so said the maulvi. Now that Amjad was at home most of the time, the children would be looked after and she could take on more work.

Amjad was used to having Shaista at home when he returned from his rounds.

"Men do not like long absences of women when they are at home. The devil begins to take hold of their head!" said one woman in the crowd.

"You mean the devil begins to take hold of their genitals!" interrupts Rubaiya candidly. The younger women giggle and cover their faces. The director of the NGO mildly rebukes Rubaiya who looks unrepentant.

One day, Shaista, unable to bear menstrual cramps, had

returned early to find the children playing out in the sun, and the house bolted from inside. She had banged on the door, all sorts of misgivings crowding into her unsuspecting mind. 'Allah let him not have committed suicide, let him still be in a stage to be saved!' A woman emerged from the house and pushed her hard. She fell but was up in a trice to find Amjad emerging out of the shanty, casually tying his pajama string. Shaista did not mind working, spending long hours away from her children, walking the two kilometers back and forth to save on the shared auto-rickshaw, coming back to cook and feed everyone before eating herself. But she did mind her hard earned money being spent on a prostitute.

In the ensuing quarrel Amjad had given all the male arguments: his needs, desires, Shaista's absence, frustration of not having work. Shaista was an honest woman scorned. Her anger and disgust could never be matched by the fury of a make-belief Hell. The result was a divorce.

Shaista was at her parents' house. Amjad had been quick to realise that he could not look after the one child he had to take care of. He had dumped the eight-year-old daughter and two sons on Shaista. He had also apologised profusely, asked her to marry someone for a day, seek a divorce, and then be back with him. Shaista was an independent working woman, yet she wanted to be back with Amjad. She still loved him. She missed the home she had created—the familiar neighbourhood and the assurance of permanent jobs. But all this had to be managed one thing at a time. She had three mouths to feed with the condition of not stepping outside her home during the period of iddat. How was that to be done? Her work was outside. At home she faced the abuses of her sister-in-law, even her own mother. With four extra mouths to feed and provide space to sleep, sit, be—their anger was understandable.

Twice, her period of iddat was cancelled because it had been reported to the local mosque that she had been seen outside her parent's home. What could she do? She had to work to feed her three children. The first time she went very early in the morning, hoping that no one would see her. But she had been seen and recognised. She had given her reasons to the questions asked but they had apparently not been good enough for the law. The second time she took care to wear a burqa. Though one of the arguments given in favour of the burqa is that it makes recognition impossible, and thus provides security for the woman, the camouflage had failed. The maulvi met her on the fifth day when she was out. When she refused to speak, he held out the Holy *Quran* asking her to swear on it that she was not Shaista. How could she do that? She broke down, wept, and on her knees had begged the maulvi to let her get through the first hurdle of the Halala. The maulvi pleaded helplessness. He has a job to see that everyone follows Islam as it has been dictated in the Book, or else everyone would begin to interpret it themselves, as per their convenience, and soon there would be innumerable versions of the *Quran*.

Somehow the first stage of iddat was completed, and then began the second and the tougher one. Where was a man to be found who would marry a mother of three and then divorce her? After all what was there in it for him? Some demanded money and this seemed the best possible arrangement, since money would be paid only when the man had fulfilled his side of the contract and pronounced the divorce. But money that had seemed so easy to save once now seemed to slip through her fingers. Fourteen months passed. Amjad got fed up of the endless wait and married another woman. Thus, Halala became useless.

Here she was with three children, no home, no support, trying to build a life out of nothing, knowing that no one would marry a mother of three for keeps.

"Temper! It is always temper!" Rubaiya gnashes her teeth. "Men are forever losing it and we women have to pay the price; sometimes tolerating physical violence, at others this kind of torture in the name of religion."

"But here it wasn't temper," says Aquila Bano. "This was temptation!" A married man decided to commit adultery. Why was he not punished for the sin? He got out of the punishment by pronouncing talaq. He not only escaped himself, he also managed to punish the woman for daring to object to his adultery.

Society has given women the right to work and earn because it has realised that doing so enhances the family's finances. Daily needs have increased making the strict social norms redundant. But has this economic self-sufficiency given the woman personal and social rights? The money Shaista earned did not give her a say in the choice of her bridegroom? Was she asked where she wanted to live? Did she have a right over how many children she would have? Did she ever get any help in managing the children and the household from her husband? Did she have the right to accept, reject or contest the Triple Talaq. Lastly, did she have any say in the manner in which she could get back her home?

Did Allah consult even a single woman when framing the laws for her?

We are told that heavens abound with angels and houries. There are records in the *Quran* of discussions between Allah and the angels. For example, right at the beginning when Allah created Adam, the male human form, from mud, he is said to have asked the angels to bow before Adam. Iblis (Satan), his favourite angel, refused and argued that when angels were made from fire why should they be obliged to bow to someone created from mud? Allah reasoned that Adam had been created resembling Allah himself. Satan still refused, was punished and thrown out of paradise. A harsh punishment meted out to the disobedient after discussion had failed.

Gabriel, till then angel number two, was elevated to position number one. There are several incidents of Gabriel being used as messenger to various Prophets, carrying out the orders and reporting back to Allah what had happened, then going back with Allah's specific instructions.

There is no account of any discussions being held with any of the houries. Naturally then there is no incident of any discussion being held with one of them and not even of angels ever conversing and discussing anything with houries.

But then Allah is a male, working overtime to promote patriarchy, and when He did not think it fit to take a woman's advice while coining the laws— why would the men, duty bound to follow Him, even think of consulting women when implementing the same laws?

Is Shaista's Case Un-Islamic?

Triple Talaq should not have been pronounced in one go, and if it was, it should have been accepted only as one. This would have given both the parties time to calm down, weigh the pros and cons, take stock of their financial position, address their grievances, have an opportunity to apologise and forgive, and have the time and space to allow counselling and advice by well wishers.

Shaista should not have been made to stay at her parents' house or any other place for the period of iddat. The *Quran* specifically says this—the whole idea being that constant presence, helping and taking care of each other's needs would make reconciliation a possibility, and talaq could be avoided.

The maulvi who was so keen to confine the woman for the period of iddat, and who moved around with the Holy Book, did not himself read, understand or follow the very clear instructions. Or else he belonged to a perverted mindset that wished to see women punished for crimes not committed.

According to the *Quran*, the eight-year-old child should have been the man's responsibility. The maulvi did not care to inform Amjad that he had no right to dump the child on Shaista. Had Shaista refused to accept the responsibility of the child she would immediately have been condemned by society as a woman with no maternal instincts. Amjad should also have been paying maintenance for the other two children till they were seven and then have taken full charge of them. This too the maulvi neither informed nor insisted on. Islam gives women very few rights and even those are not implemented.

Chapter - 5

Adultery And The Quran

'THOSE WHO commit unlawful sexual intercourse of your women—bring against them four (witnesses) from among you. And if they testify, confine the guilty women to houses until death takes them or Allah ordains for them (another) way.'

—*Quran* 4:15

Further the *Quran* says:

'The woman or man found guilty of sexual intercourse (outside nikah)—lash each one of them with a hundred lashes, and do not be taken by pity for them in the religion of Allah, if you should believe in Allah and the Last Day, and let a group of the believers witness their punishment.'

—*Quran* 24:2

Some Muslim scholars argue that the first verse was revealed to the Prophet at an early stage and then was superseded by other verses that specify the punishment. However, it is the last portion of the first verse: 'until death takes them or Allah ordains for them (another) way,' which is said to have become the basis for an adulterer being stoned to death, stoning being considered 'the way'.

God stated in the *Quran* that, for the punishment to take place, a condition is that this 'sexual' action must be witnessed by four trusted sane adults. How on earth can there be four witnesses to a sexual act? That would make it a public performance and not a hidden, concealed act of adultery. The logic for this condition is that since this is a very serious accusation in Islam, that is why Allah imposed this condition. The difficulty in providing this proof makes the hundred lashes punishment an impossibility.

Islam accepts the fact that women are in a weaker position when accusations of adultery and sexual liaisons are levelled against them. So God stated in the *Quran*: 'And those who accuse chaste women and then do not produce four witnesses—lash them with eighty lashes and do not accept from them testimony ever-after (for anything). And those are the defiantly disobedient.'

—*Quran* 24:4

However, the *Quran* quickly makes an about turn, making provision for the accusation to stand in the absence of four witnesses, or for that matter even one witness.

In case the husband is accusing his own wife of adultery, the *Quran* says: 'And those who accuse their wives and have no witnesses except themselves—then the witness of one of them (shall be) four testimonies (swearing) by Allah that indeed, he is of the truthful. And the fifth (oath will be) that the curse of Allah be upon him if he should be among the liars.'

So all that the man has to do is swear by Allah four times that he has seen his wife committing adultery and then top it up with a fifth one, inviting the curse of Allah upon himself, if he is a liar and hey presto! the accusation is accepted as the truth!

It is presumed that every Muslim man would have such a fear of Allah and would be so righteous that he would never commit the sin of swearing a lie. Was perjury unknown then? No it was not! We even have historically documented evidence of *ahl-e-bait* (Mohammad's family by blood or marriage) who have lied under oath. Allah is the all-knowing but he is also the merciful; so he shows mercy to the men who commit sins and helps them wriggle out of punishment.

On one hand, the *Quran* says that a woman shall not be punished provided she too gives four such similar testimonies by herself in a similar swearing by Allah. She can say that indeed, he, the accuser is lying and she is truthful and chaste. And the fifth oath will be that she too would invite the wrath of Allah upon herself if she was lying and he was truthful'.

—*Quran* 24: 6-9

But another interpretation in the Shariat says:

'As for the wife, if she accuses her husband of *zina* (adultery), but she cannot produce four witnesses, then she should be given the hadd punishment for slander.'

Al-Maawardi advises in *Ahkaam al-Sultaaniyyah* (p 287): 'If a woman slanders her husband, she should be given the hadd punishment, but she should not engage in Li'aan.'

Al-Qurtubi has said in his *Tafseer* (analysis): 'Allah mentioned women in the verse because they are of greater concern and accusing them of immorality is more abhorrent and more hurtful.'

What is Li'aan

Li`aan refers to a situation where a person accuses the spouse of adultery and seeks separation on this basis. This accusation and its proof can/might be an acceptable reason for divorce.

Li'aan happens in a situation where—both the accuser and the accused, have four times under oath, denied the accusation and sworn innocence. Then the accused shall not be subjected to any punishment and neither would the accuser be considered to have made a false allegation. No punishment shall be implemented upon either. The matter is then left to the couple. After such an experience, would it not become impossible to live a normal married life? If requested by either of them, the marriage is dissolved.

This divorce or separation or dissolution of marraige is Li'aan.

This reinforces the importance of this matter—that providing trusted, firm evidence is crucial.

'The repentance accepted by Allah is only for those who do wrong in ignorance (or carelessness) and then repent soon after. It is those to whom Allah will render forgiveness, and Allah is ever knowing and Wise.'

—*Quran* 4:17

But this is not what actually happens. If caught in an act of adultery, the man can get away by simply swearing his innocence. If a woman insists on establishing the fact of having been cheated and betrayed, the man can simply divorce her and the chapter is closed. The woman, even in her pain, anger and betrayal cannot divorce the man—she can only ask for khula.

What is Advised in the Scriptures

If a woman knows that her husband has committed *zina* but she has no proof, namely four witnesses, then she should advise him, and tell him to fear Allah. In other words, she has to be adjusting, generous, forgiving, compliant and accepting. She has to look the other way and not insist that she has, in any way, been cheated or deceived. This is something that women have done through the centuries. Till as recently as the middle of the last century, men from most well-to-do families in the Muslim community patronised the *kothas* or nautch girls, formed long-term liaisons and fathered children. The wife had no choice but to accept her fate and look the other way. What else could she do? According to the Shariat, she is expected to talk to him and advise him. If he persists in his sin, she may ask for a divorce from him or separate from him by means of khula. She gets nothing by staying with him, and having intercourse with him may be harmful for her because he might be the career of dangerous diseases which could be passed on to the children.

Muzammil H Siddiqi, a scholar, comments: 'There is no discrimination between a wife and husband in the case of Li'aan. If the wife accuses her husband or the husband accuses his wife, in both cases they will have to produce evidence. In the absence of evidence they have to do the Li'aan. After the Li'aan, both parties are separated. They are not husband and wife. However, if the wife accused her husband of adultery and then she refused to do the Li'aan, then in this case she will be punished for *Qadhaf* (slander). Similarly, if the husband accused his wife of adultery and then, when asked to do Li'aan he balked, then he would be punished for *Qadhaf*. Both parties are treated equally in this law. Adultery is *haraam* for a man as it is for a woman. There is no special treatment for men or women in this case.'

But What Actually Happens

A man accuses a woman of adultery, swears four times and invites Allah's wrath upon himself if he be a liar (in a fifth swear), and the accusation holds. The woman is not even asked to clarify, testify or swear innocence. She is found guilty and punished; stoning to death being the usual punishment. Thankfully in India this is not the way things proceed and end. But it has been a part of life in the Gulf, and more recently has been seen to be actively used in Nigeria, Pakistan and Afghanistan where the Hudood laws are in force.

What is Hadd or Hudood Law?

Hadd means the 'limit or prohibition'; Hudood or Hudud is the plural. These laws are punishments fixed in the *Quran* and the Hadith for crimes considered to be against God. The six crimes for which punishments are fixed—theft (amputation of the hand), illicit sexual relations (death by stoning or one hundred lashes), making unproven accusations of illicit sex (eighty lashes), drinking intoxicants (eighty lashes), apostasy (death or banishment), and highway robbery (death). Strict requirements of evidence (including eyewitnesses) have severely limited the application of Hudood penalties. Punishment for all other crimes is left to the discretion of the court. These punishments are called *tazir*. With the exception of Saudi Arabia, Hudud punishments are rarely applied, although recently fundamentalist groups have demanded the reintroduction of Hudud, especially in Sudan, Iran, and Afghanistan.

In South Asia, it was in Pakistan during the regime of General *Zia-ul-Haq* that the Hudud Ordinance came into force. While highway robbery, apostasy and theft are offences that are left outside these laws in Pakistan, mostly being committed by men (intoxication being treated mildly)—the offence of adultery is considered a major sin. Over the years the implementation of this law and prescribed punishment has taken strange and barbaric form.

Enforcement of Hudood Ordinance 1979 described the offences of *zina* (adultery) and *zina bil jabbar* (rape) separately. Prior to the Women Protection (Criminal Laws Amendment) Act 2006, the Hudood Ordinance provided for two kinds of punishments: punishments under Hadd (Section 8) or under *Tazir* (Section 10).

Under Hadd, "at least four Muslim adult male witnesses, about whom the court is satisfied as being truthful persons who abstain from major sins (*kabair*), give evidence as eye-witnesses of the act of penetration necessary to the offence."

No case could be ever proved under Hadd due to the above stringent stipulation.

Punishments until now were awarded under the *Tazir* provision of the Hudood Ordinance.

The 2006 Act has now totally deleted *zina bil jabbar* from the Hudood Ordinance and inserted Sections 375 and 376 for Rape and Punishment, respectively.

Critics of the law claim that it equates the crime of *zina* (adultery) and *zina bil jabbar* (rape). A woman alleging rape is required to provide four adult male eyewitnesses. In principal, according to the *Quran*, the failure to produce such witnesses does not place the woman herself at the risk of prosecution. However, in practice, the safeguards—that she swear four times and call Allah's wrath on herself, are not provided.

In a quirky, distorted form it is the reverse that happens. To prove rape the female victim has to state that sexual intercourse had taken place. If she is not able to produce witnesses, this statement is, in practice, viewed judicially as an admission of guilt on her part as having committed adultery, rather than as evidence of rape. If the alleged offender/offenders get acquitted for want of further evidence, the woman now faces charges for either adultery, if she is married, or for fornication, if she is not married.

There is a hidden meaning in both the cases. Note that the word *zina* occurs in both. Thus even 'rape' is a form of adultery, whereas adultery, in its very essence, is not forced like rape but is mutual. Thus even in naming the two sins, the woman has already been made a culprit in both.

According to a report by the National Commission on Status of Women (Pakistan), an estimated 80 per cent of women, in jail in 2003, were there because 'they had failed to prove rape charges and were consequently convicted of adultery'.

Stories of great personal suffering by women who claimed to have been raped appeared in the press in the years following the passing of the Hudood Ordinance. One such case was that of Safia Bibi. A blind girl, she was the victim of rape by the kiln owner and his son where she worked. She was prosecuted for the crime of *zina* because of her illegitimate pregnancy, while the rapists were acquitted. The case stirred many protests from Pakistani activists and lawyers, along with international human rights organisations. The appeal judgment of the Federal Shariah Court cleared the girl of the accusation of *zina*.

In another case, a village woman, Zafran Bibi, was pronounced guilty and the evidence of guilt was there for all to see—a newborn baby in the arms of its mother. Her crime was that she had accused the region's feudal lord of raping her. No proof in the form of four eye witnesses was possible as even her own family members had buckled under pressure from the landlord. Her sentence—death by stoning. The white-bearded judge, Anwar Ali Khan, who convicted her, said he had simply followed the letter of the *Quran*-based law, (Hudood), that mandates such punishments.

He went on to elaborate, "The illegitimate child is not disowned by her and therefore is proof of *zina*." He was referring to laws that forbid any sexual contact outside marriage. Furthermore, he said, in accusing her master of raping her, Zafran had confessed to her crime.

So Zafran should have disowned her baby, or better still killed it—hidden her lactating breasts and forgotten about the crime committed on her body, mind and soul. How did she dare to complain against the powerful, the man? How did she dare to conceive? How did she dare to give birth to the baby? She had to be punished for her own daring and to be an example for other women.

After massive protests within Pakistan and international hue and cry, Zafran Bibi, who is about twenty-six now, is in solitary confinement in a death-row cell.

However, Mufti Taqi Usmani, an instrumental figure in making the law, has stated:

"If anyone says that she was punished because of Qazaf (false accusation of rape) then Qazaf Ordinance, Clause no 3, Exemption no 2, clearly states that if someone approaches the legal authorities with a rape complaint, she cannot be punished in case she is unable to present four witnesses. No court of law can be in its right mind to award such a punishment."

Right mind or not, this is how this law is being implemented.

A number of international and Pakistani human rights organisations still campaign for the law's repeal. Some argue that it goes beyond what is required by Shariah. They are opposed by conservative religious parties, who accuse them of departing from Islamic values. The governments of Benazir Bhutto and Nawaz Sharif, both set up commissions to investigate the Hudood Ordinance. Both commissions recommended amending certain aspects of the law, but neither government followed or implemented the recommendations. They did not even initiate open discussions and debate on the subject.

The Present Status

In 2006, the then President Pervez Musharraf proposed reform of the ordinance, and on 15 November 2006, the Women's Protection Bill was passed in the Pakistan National Assembly, allowing rape to be prosecutable under civil law. The bill was ratified by the Senate on 23 November 2006, and became law after President Musharraf signed it on 1 December 2006.

The reforms have come under considerable opposition from Islamist groups in Pakistan. Other legal experts have claimed that the reforms will be impossible to enforce.

Human rights groups and activists in Pakistan have criticised the bill: "The so-called Women's Protection Bill is a farcical attempt at making the Hudood Ordinance palatable," says Asma Jehangir, human rights and democracy activist. The concern is that thousands of rapes go unreported as victims fear that they would be treated as criminals.

According to the National Commission for the Status of Women (Pakistan) and Amnesty International in Asia and the Pacific, 88 per cent of the female prisoners are in jail as a direct consequence of the Hudood Ordinance on adultery. According to statistics compiled by the Society for Advancement of Community Health Education and Training (SACHET), and Lawyers for Human Rights and Legal Aid (LHRLA) team for Karachi Women's Prison, in 2003-2004, Seven thousand women and children were languishing in 75 jails in extremely poor conditions. Human rights activists insist that the Hudood Ordinance goes against the very pronouncements of the founder of Pakistan, Muhammad Ali Jinnah, who had expressly stated that women are the equal partners of men, way back in 1944, much before the independence of India and formation of Pakistan.

In Other Countries

An Islamic court in Nigeria has upheld a sentence of death by stoning for a woman accused of adultery. The case is the latest in a series of sentences passed under Shariat law, that has been adopted over the past two years in northern regions of Nigeria, which have predominantly Muslim inhabitants.

Amina Lawal, 30, has been sentenced to death by stoning—a fate which would involve being buried up to her neck in sand, and have rocks thrown at her head. However, the Islamic court has ruled that the penalty cannot be carried out until Lawal has finished breastfeeding her baby daughter.

In sentencing Lawal, the Islamic court disregarded an earlier ruling by the federal courts, which deemed the death penalty unconstitutional for offences such as adultery.

The Supreme Court of Nigeria can most likely step in, particularly as many Shariat trials fall short of the expected standards of proof. But it faces stiff opposition from governors of Nigeria's northern states, who have made political capital out of promising a Saudi-Arabian style strictness in the adoption of Shariah, offering it to the disenfranchised poor as a way of improving their lives. In the past two years, twelve out of Nigeria's thirty-six states have adopted Shariat law.

A year ago, Safiya Hussaini, 35, was sentenced to death by stoning for allegedly having a child with a married neighbour. She had the child after her divorce, but maintained the father was her former husband and that they were married when the child was conceived. The court did not accept her version or her oaths as stipulated by the *Quran*, and convicted her. Hussaini won an appeal, this time alleging that she had sex out of wedlock. She managed to do this in the nick of time, just days before Shariat law took effect. Amina Lawal put forward a similar argument during her trial. However, the Shariat law had been adopted in the Northern region by then and her appeal was rejected by the courts.

A teenage single mother, Tariya Mohammad Magazu, was given 100 lashes for adultery, even though she argued she was raped by three men. The court said she could not prove that the men had forced her to have sex.

Adama Unusua, who is 19 and pregnant, was recently sentenced to 100 lashes for having sex with her fiancée.

Meanwhile, the sentence of Amina Lawal is provoking civil unrest, with riots breaking out between Christian and Muslim communities over how far the rule of Shariah might spread.

Acceptance of a code of law of a majority community by any state, always poses a threat to the minority community, who can never be sure of the extent to which these religious laws would interfere and erode into their personal and social identity. The most important aspect of a religious law, adopted on the national level, is whether it would remain impartial in meting out justice and pronouncing verdicts as a judiciary is expected to be.

In our immediate neighbourhood, we have seen the furore against the apprehension of Shariah being adopted as the law of the land. The people of Bangladesh were out in the streets, and Shahbagh Chowk in Dhaka became a symbol of progressive and liberal forces taking a secular stand against the possible onslaught of Jamaat-e-Islami, and their probable success in making the Shariah, the law of the land. Present in equal numbers, if not more, were women of the minority Hindu community. They were out there, because they knew just what was coming, if the fundamentalists won the day.

The issue of 'Shariah as the law of the land' is already provoking violence between Muslim and Christian communities in Nigeria, particularly in the south, where Shariat law is not in force. The previous Nigerian president, Olusegun Obasanjo, who hailed from the south, and had received significant support from northern Muslims in the last election he won, had stated that the federal government would not dispute the rights of the regional states to use Shariat Law. He has attempted to deal with the Shariah problem through compromise, by persuading courts in the north (where twelve states have begun using it) to modify their sentences. He has stated that the strict version of this law practiced in Nigeria's north was illegal under the country's constitution.

The then justice minister, in Nigeria, Godwin Agabi, wrote

to the twelve northern states which have Muslim majorities, that, "a Muslim should not be subjected to a punishment more severe than would be imposed on other Nigerians for the same offence." Agabi also noted that Nigeria "cannot be indifferent" to international outrage over the sentences.

While there is a concerted effort to bring in the Shariah in all its strict avatar, it is important to understand that there is no one version of even the Shariah, and that it can be, and is being implemented with different interpretations. Most of the countries where it is making inroads are the societies that were liberal, secular and women-friendly. Saudi Arabia is entering into pacts, one would say, with states that have Muslim populations—and on the basis of funds, donations, grants, persuading the governments to implement it.

India, being a democracy, must take a stand on this and uphold its secular, character, and be the voice of equality for men and women, so that it can be followed as an example throughout the world.

It is time to begin talking of a Uniform Civil Code, not in a majority muscle flexing, destructive manner—but calmly, with reason and logic, without threatening, but with a will to accept that a lot is wrong with religious laws and they must be viewed from a contemporary perspective. Religious communities must accept that change is a necessity for the successful growth and development of every community.

Chapter - 6

The Modern Sheherzade

Asma has come with other women. She sits, talks, eats with them. But there is a sense of alienation. In her attitude there is the self confidence of a woman who has dared to defy the conventions and come out a winner. In the others there is a grudging respect and a hidden admiration mixed with the deep rooted fear of the victorious. An apprehension. After all one does not know when the victor might set out to wage another battle, and what or who might be her target. She just might be on a path to trample others in her victory march.

She is the exception that defies the rule.

Asma was twenty-nine when she had been divorced by her husband. She had continued to breastfeed her second child, born after a gap of eight years and did not get up to make a cup of tea her mother-in-law was demanding. The first conception and delivery had been troublesome and the baby boy had been weak and sickly. Somehow the child had survived. Asma too had taken a long time to get back to normal. All this had invited a continuous flow of abuse and mistreatment from the mother-in-law who had had five children and was still as strong as an ox.

Asma had prayed that she would not conceive again soon. She became pregnant when her son was eight years old. The pregnancy had been difficult; the last three months had drained her. The labour had lasted a full forty-eight hours. The local midwife had given up after thirty hours and she had been rushed to the nearest hospital where it was another full day before the doctors decided on a cesarean.

The baby, a girl, had been healthy and pretty. But she was still a girl, and the woman who bears a girl does not deserve the same kind of care as the one who has a son. Breastfeeding meant painful spasms that racked her entire body. No help had been arranged to massage her body, wash the nappies or even bathe the baby.

"From the first day I did everything myself. From the eighth day I began to cook and serve. I tolerated everything and understood that slowly though it may be, my body would recover. I tried to finish all the chores, and sleep and wake up with the baby to give my body the much needed rest.

"My mother-in-law became wise to this arrangement and took to shouting and screaming the moment the baby had dropped off to sleep. I protested; my mother-in-law threw a tantrum. My husband was narrated the entire story by his weeping mother who asked to be sent back to her brother's house. He took her side and blamed me for always inciting quarrels.

"Now that I look back, I understand that it was he who must have become tired of me. I was still convalescing three months after the delivery—not available in bed, not able to do much cooking and other household chores. The house was no longer well kept, the elder child was neglected. From his point of view I must have seemed quite useless.

"But I ask you sisters, wasn't it his child that I had given birth to? Shouldn't he have cared for me and seen to it that I got some comfort during those trying months? Is the man's sexual need and desire foremost, to be assuaged at whatever cost to the woman? With good food and adequate rest I would have got well in a couple of months, and then have taken care of all his needs. It was only a matter of time. What is so wrong with having a daughter? How would he have come into this world had it not been for a woman? And why didn't my mother-in-law treat me with kindness? Some women give birth as easily as they change their clothes, others have a tough time in each delivery; some even die in labour. Can a woman be held responsible for her physical condition?"

Asma asked all these questions and the women sitting around her nodded in agreement.

Then she brought out a silver box of shredded betel nut and cardamoms and passed it around; when everyone had the hunger subdue in their mouths, she continued, "The climax came on that day. My daughter had been running fever for the past three days. She had hardly taken a few mouthfuls of milk. Since morning she had been a bit better and in the afternoon had begun to hold my breast, trying to suckle it through the *kameez*. My breasts had become swollen and I had been massaging them to begin the flow of milk. I had been awake three nights trying to keep her quiet so that my husband and son could sleep. I thought if she took a full feed, she would sleep and I would also be able to rest for an hour before my son came back from school. Just as the baby started sucking and I felt relief and a drowsiness overtaking me, my mother-in-law yelled that it was an hour since she had had her lunch and wasn't anyone going to give her a cup of tea. I tried to feign sleep hoping that she would keep quiet at least till the baby had been fed. But no. She first yelled at me, then yelled to inform the neighbourhood what a lazy, good-for-nothing daughter-in-law she had. I begged her to keep quiet till I had fed the baby and that did it. She began sobbing that I had told her to shut up.

"In the evening, my husband was narrated the incident with many juicy details. He came into our room and said that he was fed up with the constant bickering in the house. I tried to make him understand my side of the story but seeing the happy, playful, laughing baby, he questioned why she could not be left hungry for five minutes, which would have been enough to make a cup of tea.

"He went out and I thought he wanted to take a walk to cool down. I prepared tea and came to the drawing room with a loaded tray only to find him sitting with two men. My husband had never been very religious. He had never insisted that I wear the veil and had seldom attended the Friday jamaat (gathering or congregation) for prayers himself. In fact he had often joked that his belief leaned more towards atheism than towards Islam or any religion. I was a bit surprised to see a bearded gentleman and it took me a minute to realise that he was a maulvi.

"My husband took the tray from me and put it down on the centre table and then said, 'Asma Bano, daughter of Hasan Waheed, I divorce you now in the presence of these two witnesses'."

One of the older women in the crowd stood up. "What is new in this? It is a repetition of our stories with slight differences. We have all gone through this. Tell us the main thing—how did you survive the Halala."

I looked at her in surprise. Survived Halala! Now how had she managed to do that?

"I am coming to that. I was packed off to my parents for the iddat. My daughter died. Maybe she had not really recovered from the sickness—maybe because the shock of the sudden divorce had dried up the milk and I had still not weaned her to the bottle. Maybe she was just not a being of this earth. Whatever it might have been, my husband, when he heard this news, began to suffer from pangs of guilt and remorse. He came to me, all prepared. He had persuaded a close friend Hanif to marry me and then divorce me after a night. I had met Hanif. I liked him as a person. He was soft-spoken and unmarried. He came from a good family. I agreed.

"After the nikah, we were left alone. Both of us felt awkward. He had always called me *Bhabhi*. To put him at ease I began to talk about this strange system—about women being treated as a commodity, about the trampling of a woman's emotions and also how this was against Islam. We discussed through the night; discussed—not argued. He said that it was an instruction; I pointed out that it had been vastly distorted. He accepted this logic but still maintained that the custom had survived so many centuries. I put forward the plea that just because something had lasted a long time did not mean that it was right. The discussion went on and on. I was so exhausted that I almost gave up. But something kept me going. I still do not know what it was that gave me the strength and the intelligence to keep on contesting every argument that he put forward. Was it the wish to live with dignity? Was it facing the injustice of the way a woman has to accept everything as 'her fate'? Even today I cannot be certain what it was.

"At dawn Hanif said, 'Both of us understand that we are being used; me for a night, you forever. But what is to be done? How can we change a system that has taken such deep roots that it is now part of religion, even though it goes against its fundamentals?'

"Well I do not know about the system or the religion but you can certainly change things for me."

"How?" Hanif asked.

"Do not divorce me today, and promise me, that even though we are Sunni Muslims, you shall never pronounce the Triple Talaq in one go."

"He said, 'I had been meaning to make this suggestion to

you, but I wanted you to be free to make the choice. Now that you have decided, we are together forever.' Then he hugged me. I had never been hugged that way. That hug told me I had found my soul mate."

This was a modern day Sheherzade—the woman who had saved her own life and the life of so many others from the brutal Sultan bent on avenging the betrayal of one woman by taking revenge on every woman he married. She had been able to make the Sultan see reason and logic through her stories. This modern one had used logic and reason to rewrite her own story.

"So now that you have managed to beat the system why are you here?"

"I am an individual. My victory does not defeat the system. I want everyone to get justice and that is why I am here—to lend my voice to the demand that the system needs to be changed."

Asma's was a chance victory. She knew Hanif and had gambled. It just might not have paid off. Hanif might have had his satisfaction through the night and still divorced her. Or he might not have done so for several weeks, months, years and then pronounced the talaq one day, suddenly out of the blue. One could say that fate had supported her and she was most fortunate.

"So you are here because you want that the system of pronouncing Triple Talaq in one sitting be changed?" I questioned her over tea.

"That is right," she says with a confident smile.

"And you also want the practice of Halala to be given up.

"Yes that too! And the rest!"

"The rest?"

"Well there is a lot that is wrong with Islamic laws. I guess there must be flaws in other religious laws as well. But then that is not my concern. I have read and reread the *Quran*; I have read through the *Surah-e-Nisa* (portion on women and property) several times,

I have also studied the Shariat Laws and have understood the *Muslim Personal Law*. With each study my belief has become firmer that a lot needs to be re-examined, re-considered, debated and changed."

As she spoke I recalled the face of the Muslim scholar from Andhra Pradesh. It was a meeting for the planning of a Sufi conference. The preparatory meet should have been amongst scholars of Sufism and Bhakti and not scholars of Islam. But then blurring of divisions and overlapping of compartments is a part of democracy.

When it was his turn to speak, this scholar made a statement that there never was, nor is there a need today for exploring the various paths of devotion and worship. Everything was made very clear in the Holy *Quran* and there was no necessity to explore any further. With one stroke he had negated the very need for holding this conference. Then he had continued (perhaps taking a dig at me and a couple of other women present), "My wife religiously reads the *Quran* every day. But she does not understand it. I am always telling her that just reading is not enough—she should understand it and then follow it."

When it was my turn to speak I began by congratulating the gentleman that he possessed such a religious wife who performed *talawat* (reading the *Quran*) everyday without fail. He swelled up with pride. "But there is more for which you should be congratulated. You should thank your lucky stars that your wife only reads the *Quran* but does not understand it. If she was to fully comprehend it, she would know the way she has been treated by this benevolent and merciful Allah, this God of the entire Universe (Rab-e-la-ameen). And having realised this, she, with the knowledge that God has been both partial and patriarchal, would set about reforming and changing the law to give herself and other women a fair and just deal."

Chapter - 7

Multiple Wives And Islam

Scholars of Islam maintain that the *Quran* clearly gives the correct method for obtaining divorce, stretching over three months. If that is followed and made mandatory there would be no Halala issue at all. But is it likely to happen? Once a legal process of allowing men to satisfy their lust has come into being, there is no way of making them go back, short of completely doing away with it. Even after the divorce in three months and the wife going away, the man might want her back. This he is allowed to consider even though he may have married again. He can keep the second wife and also get back the first one. But there is an important twist here, and with that twist comes the second important issue—should men be allowed more than one wife at a time?

In this, even the liberal, progressive Muslim men who profess to be on the side of the women have a warped mindset.

A senior scholar with a Left leaning had fallen in love with a young dancer. He was twice her age and married with three children. Before anyone begins to find hidden meanings in the girl being a 'dancer', it must be clarified that she was highly educated, with a masters in philosophy. She was the only daughter of liberal, progressive parents and had come in contact with this gentleman through her Leftist friends. He was a good speaker with a thorough knowledge of the Marxist text and a clear understanding of contemporary politics. She had been dancing since she was eight, wished to pursue it as a career but was being pressurised by her family 'to settle down'—this phrase having just one meaning in South Asia—that the girl should get married. Sahiba wanted someone who would let her dance, not insist on having children—something which takes away years from a woman's life and vigour from her body. Dilshad accepted her logic and was willing to marry her on her terms. But Sahiba put a condition. She refused to be the second wife. Dilshad would have to divorce his first wife and then marry her.

Years later, another comrade while discussing women's rights had narrated this story as an example of women being their own worst enemies. When asked to elaborate he had said that Sahiba should have married Dilshad without insisting that he divorce his first wife. This, according to the comrade, was cruel of her and unjust of Dilshad to have accepted the condition. So this comrade was not accusing Dilshad of having an extra marital affair; he also had nothing to say against the fact that Sahiba was Dilshad's daughters age—but was upset at the fact that he went through the legal procedure of breaking a relationship before legally forming another. Sahiba's stand was straightforward and direct. She had no problem with Dilshad paying the meher and also the maintenance of his three daughters. But she did not want to be married to a man who could jump out of her bed and walk into another woman's bedroom. When she was willing to be tied to one man, why shouldn't the man do the same and be committed to one woman?

Sahiba and Dilshad's marriage did not last beyond a couple of years. Following the divorce, Dilshad wanted to return to his first wife, who was willing to forgive and forget and marry him again. But that was not a possibility. They could not be legally married till she had been married to someone else. The first wife was not willing to accept this. She did not wish to be married, even for a short time, to someone she did not know, did not like, but had to tolerate so that she could get back to the one she knew, liked and wanted to spend the rest of her life with. Dilshad tried to talk this over with Muslim scholars but was told that the *Quran* was very specific in this, and the instruction was that the woman should be married again, and then divorced to become halal for the first husband.

So one is left wondering what should be addressed first and from where should one begin to solve this problem—from the Triple Talaq, from the fact that the system of Halala has been so rigidly laid down, or that Islam allows four wives in one go—from nikah being a detailed contract but talaq being verbal, or *fatwa*s being issued left, right and centre, and most importantly, in the social and moral pressure on the spouses to accept and obey the *fatwas*.

Yes Asma is right. There is a lot that is wrong with Islamic laws. Whatever had been left undefined or unstipulated has been made watertight by the Shariat. Add to this the tribal traditions that had their own forms of subjugation of the women and one finds that Islam is a religion that seems to have been avenging itself on women through the ages.

The arrangement prescribed by the *Quran*, and upheld by Shariat, has no sensitivity towards the woman as a human being. It works on the premise, that a man's wife sleeping with another man would be such a big deterrent for the husband, that no man in his right senses would divorce his wife. The 'untouched, virginity syndrome' that every man is expected to suffer from, would see to it that a man does not divorce his wife without due contemplation.

But this deterrent does not seem to be working. The Triple Talaq has increased manifold in the last three decades. Halala also has become more frequent, taking place usually for two reasons: the man genuinely regrets his act and wants to make amends, or when there are no other options available. Since there are always women who are too poor, too desperate, or getting on in years, who would marry a once-divorced man, the question of no other option being available seldom arises.

Why does a man want the woman, his first wife, back. Usually it is because the new bride does not wish to be saddled with the first woman's offsprings. She wants to have her own children or finds the housework and looking after the children too much labour. Perhaps the man is missing the companionship he had developed with his first wife—after all she had got used to his needs and used to make that extra effort to fulfill them.

The law does not say that both of them should marry someone else. It specifically states that the woman has to be married again and divorced. The man might have married again, might have divorced the second wife or the second wife might have died, yet he cannot come back to the first one legally. It is she who should be married again, be divorced or become a widow, to be able to marry her first husband again.

But what of the woman? Does she not have any feelings or emotions? Would she wish to come back to a man who treats her like an old shoe? Chucking it away because he is tired of it but then wanting it back because it had become comfortable through use! Can the woman forget that she had been abused through one night by a stranger, whose only aim was to satisfy his lust and throw her out again? How would she ever live with the first man, sleep with him, bear more children, knowing that he could do this again and again and repeatedly subject her to this indignity?

Liberal Muslim scholars advise that men and women should not accept divorce as legal until it has been pronounced on three separate occasions with the stipulated gap in-between the pronouncements. No matter how many times the husband pronounces divorce the first time, it would be considered only one divorce, after which coming together was a possibility. They insist that if this were made clear to the couple, (that) this evil custom would come to an end.

They maintain that this evil is basically a result of a craftily devised mullah conspiracy to fulfill their own vile desires.

The most worrying aspect of this practice is that the corrupt muftis and mullahs have promoted this practice to satisfy their own lust for having sex with multiple women, without fear of condemnation or opposition, either from their own wives or from society.

Yes, Asma had read, studied and understood the *Quran*. She knows that seldom are men so honest and forthright as her Hanif, and seldom do women have the knowledge or courage to take on the *Quran* or the Shariat. So she is out, not to just fight against the injustice of Triple Talaq and Halala, but also other laws that are grossly unfair to women.

Chapter - 8

From Tribal Liberalism To Fundamentalist Monotheism

Defenders of the *Quran* argue that it was sent to suit any time and any place. Since societies keep changing and norms for civilization can never be static, this insistence on its suitability for any time and place has left the door open for confused interpretations and guess work. Many Muslim scholars argue that the sources of Shariat law are the *Quran*, the Sunnah (which is anything the Prophet did and must be followed by Muslims), and the Hadith (the sayings of the Prophet). But what if the *Quran* has two different instructions about the same deed or sin?

What if the *Quran* had stated one thing but the Prophet had chosen to act differently? There are incidents that have been recorded which show this. In the case of Shariat, the choice has consistently been anti-women.

It is said that in one incident of adultery, the Prophet ordered the stoning to death of the culprit—a woman. This incident is now taken as standard punishment for adultery and incorporated in the Shariat.

But did the Prophet have the right to change God's words? God told the Prophet in the *Quran*: 'Follow that which is inspired in thee from thy Lord.'

—*Quran* 6:106

And *Quran* nowhere prescribes stoning to death as punishment for adultery.

Then God told his believers: 'Follow that which is sent down unto you from your Lord, and follow no protecting friends besides Him. Little do ye recollect!'

—*Quran* 7:3.

So again and again, the Muslims are being instructed to follow the word of the *Quran*.

Do these Muslim scholars suggest that the same God, whom they claim to be perfect, has forgotten to include this particular punishment in the *Quran*, and therefore, the Prophet had updated it?

And how come when God, the most gracious and merciful, set a punishment to be lashing, the Prophet increased it to stoning until death, though God said: 'We sent thee not, but as a Mercy for all creatures.'

—*Quran* 21:107

In another twist to the adultery punishment, the *Quran* states: 'And whoever among you cannot (find) the means to marry free, believing women, then (he may marry) from those whom your right hands possess of believing slave girls. And Allah is most knowing about your faith. You (believers) are of one another. So marry them with the permission of their people and give them their due compensation according to what is acceptable. They should be chaste, neither (of) those who commit unlawful intercourse randomly nor those who take (secret) lovers. But once they are sheltered in marriage, if they should commit adultery, then for them is half the punishment for free (unmarried) women. This (allowance) is for him among you who fears sin, but to be patient is better for you. And Allah is Forgiving and Merciful.'

—*Quran* 4:25.

This is a clear instruction for men who had moved towns or shifted place of residence, were soldiers in armies that were waging long wars in other countries, or were undertaking long travels for trade or business.

The point to be noted here is that if the punishment by either lashing or stoning was meant to kill the sinner, and if full punishment would apply to some while half of the punishment to another, depending on their social and marital status—how could you punish one with death and another with half death?

The *Quran*, in a very far reaching instruction, states a different number of lashes based on the marital status of the culprit. If the man and the woman are single then the number of lashes will be less than if they were married. This is because married people can access sexual intercourse with their partners, but unmarried people can't be stripped of their desires, and as human beings they commit mistakes. Therefore, the number of lashes is less as punishment for them.

The idea of lashing, harsh as it is, was meant to deter those who are considered sinners —to purify them and not by any means lead to death. There are conditions for the lashing. The person who performs the lashes must use soft material and is banned from using metal. He must not raise his arm high, but to the middle so no one can see under his arm, which means the lashes will be medium and not strong. The punished people are supposed to stay fully clothed so the effect of the lashes is lessened.

So where did this idea of stoning or lashing till death come from? Allah stated: 'Whoever kills a soul unless for a soul or for corruption (done) in the land—it is as if he had slain mankind entirely.'

—*Quran* 5:32

The significance of this verse reflects the importance of human life for God and contradicts any support, based on the *Quran*, about stoning till death.

The scholars of *Quran* and Islam claim that this religion established order, peace and equality among the Arab tribes who were constantly at war with each other over pasturelands, watering holes, caravan routes etc. More than that, they insist that women were being given a very tough deal. The women did not have any rights to ancestral property. The Arabs were also given to killing newborn baby girls, usually burying them alive in hot sand, because they did not wish to be saddled with a being that could be looted and thus, bring humiliation and degradation to the tribe and clan.

Much is made of the marriage being a contract between two willing parties in Islam. The union of two individuals is not considered as made in heaven or decided by God. It is something in which people have a say, and because it is a voluntary decision it can also be broken and ended. It is said that Islam was the first religion that brought the concept of divorce to humanity.

The first thing then that needs to be done is to examine the pre-Islamic era.

How is it possible that women did not have a right to ancestral property? There are several examples of women handling finances and conducting lucrative businesses all by themselves. Hazrat Khadija, the Prophet's first wife, was a successful business woman. An important entrepreneur, she traded with neighbouring countries sending out goods caravans and finalising deals with cross-border traders. It was to accompany a trade caravan to Syria that Mohammad was engaged. Khadija was in possession of wealth and one wonders where she got the capital to invest in this business. Surely at least a part of it must have been inherited, since there is no record of her starting life penniless.

This is much before Islam was revealed to Prophet Mohammad—actually fifteen years before. And Khadija, being much older than the Prophet, had been conducting this business for almost two decades. There are other examples like hers and all of them go to prove that not only did women inherit, they also enjoyed the freedom to use the money and invest it in whichever way they liked.

So Islam having brought independence to women is a completely false belief.

Next point in the pro-Islam propaganda is that in the pre-Islam era Arabs killed their daughters. But one finds that every senior sahaba (Prophet's companions) had three to four wives and grown up children showing that they possessed these wives for several years before Islam came into being. How can the presence of so many young and middle-aged women around be accounted for if all female babies were being killed?

This was probably a custom in a small group or sub-clan and Mohammad made them stop this barbaric tradition; which is certainly an act to be admired. However it cannot be generalised for the entire Arab society.

Islam was the first religion to introduce divorce to humanity.

This is a completely false statement. Divorce was prevalent in the Arab tribes, as in most of the pagan tribal societies where women enjoyed a certain level of equality. Tribal law all over Asia accepts the right of the individual to walk out of a relationship. This is true for both men and women. Khadija, the Prophet's first wife, was herself a divorced woman before she married Mohammad. On the contrary, Islam, far from giving this right to Muslim women, has made it impossible for a woman to divorce her husband.

Before Islam, Arab women could also divorce their husbands by the simple pronouncement of the word 'talaq' and they would use an idol, (Hubal, Manat etc) to legitimise the divorce. Today it is difficult for a Muslim woman in a Muslim country to get a divorce. In a situation where a woman can no longer remain married to her husband, and all attempts to save the marriage have failed, the ideal solution would be for her to obtain a divorce from the husband. The husband, seeing that the marriage is futile and there is no hope of reconcilement, should also issue a divorce according to the prescribed method in the Shariah. Whatever the case may be, it has to be the husband who pronounces divorce. The woman might have lived for years away from her husband, yet she would neither be considered a divorcee nor could she utter the word 'talaq' and be free of the tie.

Not only can the woman not get a divorce on her own, the *Quran* also provides the man with the right to demand payment for divorcing her.

However, in the case where the husband refuses to issue a divorce, the wife may persuade the husband to enter into an agreement of khul (a release for payment from the wife). The wife may also opt to exempt the husband from paying her dowry (meher).

One is not contesting that women, in the pre-islamic era, might have been badly treated; but Islam did not in anyway better their position. Rather, it set down a complete doctrine that would have to be adhered to and that did not allow the possibility of any change in the position of the woman.

With monotheism, which came to the region with Abraham and Zoroaster, patriarchy became the dominant social system. We need to differentiate between the patriarchal set-up of the tribes that divided labour for survival and the one that was propagated to subjugate the woman. The former took into consideration the female physique, her major role in reproduction, long involvement in breastfeeding and child rearing. Thus men took on the jobs of hunting, of tilling the land, grazing the animals, managing the markets and providing security. Since women were the chief procreators, hence female deities were often the supreme one for tribes and clans.

But transition from a female God to a male one was only a matter of time. While historical evidence is available of female prophets in Arabia and of women being high priestesses of reigning deities, monotheism set about systematically taking away this role and other rights of women. The process of denying woman any religious position was completed in Islam, which is why it is in a way the culmination of patriarchy.

The rights of the women were taken away and male ownership of property was turned into law. Since Arabs were still in the process of settling down from their nomadic life, a large portion of *Quran* is dedicated to treatment of friends, neighbours, social living patterns and most specifically to women. Used to a certain amount of freedom that the nomadic life style allowed, the women would not have easily acquiesced their independence. Hence there was an emphasis on good women, house restrictions, distance from men, lack of entertainment, restriction on music and dance.

Inspite of all these bindings, there are certain rights given to the woman vis-a-vis property, acceptance in marriage, right to meher, acquisition of knowledge, and a few more. A hundred and fifty years after the death of Prophet Mohammed, Islam has spread far and wide. It has come in contact with much more developed societies and civilisations that have been developing their culture, arts, science, mathematics, medicine and architecture, for centuries. Slowly these culturally stronger civilisations began to influence Islam, and the progressive, liberal face of the religion began to emerge. This was naturally not acceptable to the Arabs. A century and a half after Mohammad, the Shariat was coined and became the mainstay of the Arabic Islam.

Though Shariat had been coined and accepted in the Arab world it had still not been accepted in most of the Islamic world. From the Persian Gulf had emerged, what is said to be, an offshoot of Islam called Sufism. All the places where Sufism spread, were or had been, Buddhist for a long time (Gandhara, Kushan, Central Asia). Buddhism in itself promoted a kind of atheism that allowed an individual the space to explore and to create their own worship.

So for a good eight centuries Islam continued in its liberal, broadly plural avatar. Then came along Wahhabi, and in quick succession oil was found in the Gulf region.

Chapter - 9

The Rise Of Wahhabism

"But it does not happen very often. After all, how many cases are you taking up? Eight or nine? See, seldom do such incidents happen!"

This came from an educated, progressive Muslim woman. She is also a fellow writer and writes about women's issues. She was participating with me in a panel discussion on rights of Muslim women when this is what she quipped in her high-pitched voice.

'This is not your line, you moron!' I longed to shout at her. 'In my script this was a man's line.' But then, down the ages, women have been the pillars of patriarchy, which would never have survived had it not been for women accepting it as the legitimate social arrangement.

'Few and far between' is the usual argument given by the 'no change needed ever' groups. Supporters of this view believe that incidents like this happen so rarely that they really do not matter. But just because these cases are few in number, should they be allowed to occur with no resistance offered? Why should even a single woman in a progressive, liberal, democratic society have to suffer this kind of humiliation and injustice?

Also what is to stop this becoming a frequent occurrence? Triple Talaq too was not very common a century back; Neither was stoning to death or public whipping—and so many other things that have now become a daily occurrence in the Islamic world.

But this lady had got her figures wrong in the first place. Social activists have been collecting data and they claim that cases of Triple Talaq, followed by Halala, have multiplied at least ten times in the last decade. Some women have now dared to talk about it. But there is an equal number, if not more, who do not acknowledge it. They wish to forget and want the people around them to forget also.

When and how did these customs, that had not changed or revised, and were socially looked down upon, begin to resurface?

Religious reforms that took place in India in the 19th and early 20th centuries had brought about certain social changes that gave a limited amount of freedom and dignity to the women. Drastic changes that were happening in the social fabric of the colonial rulers had their repercussions in the colonies—modern education, influence of philosophers like Karl Marx, western literature and the Russian revolution had a deep impact on the Indian subcontinent. These ushered in an era of acceptance of plurality of thought, ideology, and most importantly, a movement towards the narrowing of the huge mental gap that was the accepted social and religious norm between genders.

The loosening of the grip of colonial powers and the discovery of petrol happened more or less simultaneously. By the time the independence of colonies arrived, holdings in the petroleum fields had become the major source of power.

With petroleum came the petro dollars, and Saudi Arabia, an unproductive land, with practically no cultural, social or civilisational history, became one of the richest states in the world almost overnight. Armed with these riches and possessing the Mecca and Medina, the Saudis now set out on a crusade to change the Islamic world into a Wahhabi world. The Wahhabi ideology does not concern itself with just the existing Muslims, but aims to convert the whole world to Islam.

What Is Wahhabism?

Wahhabism or *Wahhābiyyah*, in Arabic, can be defined as a religious movement that developed out of Sunni Islam and grew into a sect. It has been variously described as 'orthodox', 'ultra-conservative', 'propagating austerity', 'fundamentalist' and 'puritanical'. In its inception it was an Islamic 'reform movement' that aimed to restore 'pure monotheistic worship'. Wahhabism aspires to return to the earliest fundamental Islamic sources of the *Quran* and the Hadith, with inspiration from the teachings of medieval theologian, Ibn Taymiyyah, and early jurist, Ahmad ibn Hanbal.

Wahhabism was a revivalist movement that was initiated by an eighteenth century theologian, Muhammad ibn Abd al-Wahhab (1703–1792) from Najd, Saudi Arabia.

Who Was Muhammad Ibn Abd-Al-Wahhab?

Born in Najd in what is now Saudi Arabia, Mohammad ibn Abd-al-Wahhab studied in Basra and is reported to have developed his ideas there. He is also reported to have studied in Mecca and Medina while he was there to perform Hajj before returning to his home town of 'Uyayna' in 1740.

In Uyayna, a town in the region of Najd, he began teaching and attracted a large number of followers, including the ruler of the town, Uthman ibn Mu'ammar. He eventually convinced, Uthman ibn Mu'ammar, to help him in his struggle to reinstate

Islam in all its initial glory. It seems that he wanted a revenge for the way the Muslims had been defeated, and the major portion of Europe reconquered by the Christian armies during the Great Crusade. Having got the support of the local ruler he began to carry out some of his religious reforms, that included the levelling of the grave of Zayd ibn al-Khattab, who was one of the companions of Prophet Muhammad. He is also said to have judged an adultress and ordered her stoning to death. These actions were disapproved of by Sulaiman ibn Muhammad ibn Ghurayr of the tribe of Bani Khalid, the chief of Al-Hasa, and Qatif, who held substantial influence in Najd, and Ibn Abd-al-Wahhab was expelled from Uyayna.

On his banishment he was invited to settle in neighbouring Diriyah by its ruler Muhammad ibn Saud (whose two brothers had been his students), in 1740. Upon arriving in Diriyya, a pact was made between Ibn Saud and Ibn Abd-al-Wahhab, by which the latter pledged to implement and enforce Wahhab's teachings, while himself remaining the temporal 'leader' of the movement.

The Saudi Amir created space for this movement that gained unchallenged precedence in most of the Arabian Peninsula. This pact provided political and financial power for the religious revival represented by Ibn Abd al-Wahhab and created the Kingdom of Saudi Arabia, where Wahhab's teachings became the state-sponsored and dominant form of Islam.

As part of the alliance, Ibn Abd-al-Wahhab, trained and prepared the Saudi army, inculcating in the soldiers the belief that the war they would fight would be a Jehad. He promised them paradise on martyrdom, and wealth of the loot from victories.

From the last years of the 18th century, Ibn Saud and his heirs mounted various military campaigns to seize control of Arabia and its outlying regions.

One of their most famous and controversial attacks was on Karbala in 1802 (1217 AH). There, according to a Wahhabi chronicler, `Uthman b `Abdullah b Bishr:

The Wahhabi jehadis scaled the walls, entered the city and killed the majority of its people in the markets and in their homes. They destroyed the dome placed over the grave of Hazrat Husain and looted whatever they found inside the dome and its surroundings. They plundered the mausoleum, including the grille surrounding the tomb which was encrusted with emeralds, rubies, and other jewels, destroyed different types of property, weapons, clothing, carpets, ornaments of gold, silver, and precious copies of the *Quran*.

Their raids and conquests of smaller kingdoms, feudal states and tribal land continued for almost a century.

In 1818, they were defeated by the Ottoman forces. But after the collapse of the Ottomon empire, the Arabs seized control of Hijaz and the Arabian peninsula, safeguarding their vision of Islam. In the process they founded Saudi Arabia as a nation, based around the tenets of Islam as preached by Muhammad ibn Abd al-Wahhab. By the end of the 19th century, Saudi Arabia and its Amir were the rulers of the biggest region in West Asia, and Wahhabism was officially declared the state religion.

The Saudi government established the Commission for the Promotion of Virtue and Prevention of Vice—a state religious police unit, to enforce religiously conservative rules of behaviour.

The movement claims to adhere to the correct understanding of the general Islamic doctrine of Tawhid, on the 'uniqueness' and 'unity' of God, shared by the majority of Islamic sects. But it claims to rely on the *Quran* and the Hadith, without any speculative philosophy, so as not to transgress beyond the limits of the early Muslim converts. It attacked a 'perceived moral decline and political weakness' in the Arabian Peninsula and condemned what it perceived as idolatry—the popular cult of saints, and shrines and tomb visitations, advocating a purging of the widespread practices that it considered as 'impure'.

The terms Wahhabi and Salafi and *ahl al*-hadith (people of hadith) are often used interchangeably, but Wahhabism is a particular orientation that is ultra-conservative and which rejects traditional Islamic legal scholarship.

So Wahhabi ideology rejects sufis and saints—the people who acted as bridges between communities, preached plurality and peaceful coexistence, and created secular spaces that offered solace and were patronised by all religions and sects. But it also rejects the revisiting and re-analysis of the Islamic law as something that may lead to a recoining of the legal system dictated by the *Quran*, Hadith and Sunnah.

Wahhabism claims to be a revivalist movement that aims to bring Muslims back from what it believes are foreign accretions that have corrupted Islam. It also believes that Islam is a complete way of life that does not require any further exploration and knowledge. But it does not just stop at preaching this, or attracting followers to its fold through dialogue and discussion. It is quite strict in what it considers Islamic behaviour. For example, all Muslims are expected to abstain from alcohol, dress modestly, and offer prayers five times a day. But for Wahhabis, prayer has to be punctual, ritually correct, and communally performed. This is not only urged but is publicly required of men. Not only is wine forbidden, but so are 'all intoxicating drinks and other stimulants, including tobacco'. Not only is modest dress prescribed, but the type of clothing that should be worn, especially by women—a black abaya, covering everything but the eyes and hands is specified.

Practices that have been forbidden by Wahhabi preachers include performing or listening to music, dancing, fortune telling, wearing of amulets, watching television programes unless they are religious and about Islam, smoking, playing backgammon, chess or cards, drawing human or animal figures, acting in a play or writing fiction, (both of which are considered forms of lying), dissecting cadavers, even in criminal investigations or for the purposes of medical research. The list goes on and on. Common Muslim practices that Wahhabis believe are contrary to Islam include listening to music in praise of Muhammad, or in worship, visiting tombs including the tomb of Prophet Muhammad, celebrating his birthday, building of minarets or the use of ornamentation, on or in mosques.

But there are some double standards. The tomb of Mohammad remains the most visited site after the Kaaba. Majority of people going for Hajj make a visit to this tomb—a grand mausoleum. Both for financial and religious reasons, the Saudi Arabs shall never propose any harm to this monument, however un-islamic it might be. Saudi Arabia has continuously been providing funds for the construction of grand mosques, not just within their own country but also in other countries. The Faisal mosque in Islamabad—a huge mosque with tall minarets, white marble and beautiful decor is one example. The Taliban, who claim to be strict Wahhabis, practice dream interpretation, something that is abhorred in Wahhabism. But laws for women are strictly implemented. The driving of motor vehicles by women is allowed in every country except Wahhabi-dominated Saudi Arabia, the head-to-toe black cover is a must, and the death sentence and flogging of women on pressing charges for rape and sexual harassment are common practices.

Coercion is used to enforce the following of Shariah, through an official committee empowered to 'Command the Good and Forbid the Evil'. This committee has developed a security force that is known as the 'religious police' in Saudi Arabia. Scholars of Wahhabism dominate many aspects of the kingdom's life. Committee field officers enforce strict closing of shops at prayer time, segregation of the sexes, prohibition of the sale and consumption of alcohol, driving of motor vehicles by women, and other social restrictions.

Wahhabism emphasizes Thaqafah Islamiyyah or Islamic culture, and the importance of avoiding non-Islamic cultural practices, no matter how innocent they may be—on the grounds that the Sunnah forbids imitating non-Muslims. Foreign practices, sometimes punished, and sometimes simply condemned by Wahhabi preachers as unIslamic, include celebrating foreign festivals, shaving, cutting or trimming of beards, presenting of flowers, standing up in someone's honour, celebrating birthdays including the Prophet's and keeping or petting dogs.

Wahhabism puts great store on behaviour and appearance. Robes for men long enough to cover the ankles are considered an example of unseemly pride, although not forbidden. But for a woman to be seen with a robe that shows her ankles, even if they are covered in socks, is forbidden and punishable.

Wahhabis believe that the different physiological structure and biological functions of the different genders means that each sex is assigned a different role within the family. As a consequence, Wahhabis believe Islam forbids wives travelling or working outside the home without their husband's permission—permission which may be revoked at any time.

Despite this strictness, senior Wahhabi scholars of Islam in the Saudi kingdom have made notable exceptions in ruling on what is *haraam*. For example, foreign non-Muslim troops are forbidden in a crusade for Islam. But they were allowed when the king needed them to confront Saddam Hussein in 1990; then the non-muslim troops not only fought on the side of the Saudis, they were also allowed other liberties like drinking, and bathing almost naked in the sea, in full public view. Mixing of men and women is forbidden, and fraternisation with non-Muslims is discouraged, but not at King Abdullah University of Science and Technology, where most teachers are non-Muslims. After vigorous debate and international pressure, religious authorities allowed the use of paper money in 1951, the abolition of slavery in 1962, education of females in 1964, and the use of a personal television in 1965.

According to some observers, since the late 1990s and first decade of 2000, a split has developed in the Wahhabi/Salafi movement between those who support obedience to the House of Saud on the one hand, and those who focus on jehad(Salafist jehadists) against the US and (what they believe) are other enemies of Islam, supporting a removal of the House of Saud.

Chapter - 10

Halala Fixing
A Lucrative Business

The organisations working with the Muslim community and addressing issues related to women inform that Halala is on the increase. Not only has the frequency increased but it can now be found in different economic strata of the society. Most frightening is the fact that it has begun to surface in all sorts of distorted, perverted forms.

In a Jansunvai (public hearing), a woman has come with a young man. She is about thirty-five, he in his early twenties. The young man makes her stand aside, and offers through gestures to get her a chair. She refuses and asks him to hurry. The man is dressed in jeans and a shirt. She is wearing a burqa but has overturned the naqab and left her face uncovered. She is looking around confidently and without any awkwardness. The man walks from one group to another. He spends a couple of minutes with each group. The shaded lawn of the Town Hall of Bareilly is fairly crowded, and most of the crowd seems to be made up of religious Muslim men sporting a beard and above-ankle pyjamas. The young man seems to be trying to insist on something but no one is interested.

Zainab had been watching the young man—the fruitless efforts he was making, the open curiosity with which the woman was eyed, the shaking of heads and rejection of his pleas. Zainab was also watching the woman who was watching the young man. Her eyes following him were steadfast, holding a silent faith that came from knowing she was right.

Zainab, a young journalist, had been very enthusiastic about the entire concept of Jansunvais, and the way women were now getting a voice. The young man was walking up to the woman after the fifth rejection, when Zainab stepped up, and introducing herself, took them both to one side hoping to hear the story. She had a gut feeling that this woman was being purposely pushed aside. Maybe what she had to say would become an embarrassment for the rest of the community. Her curiosity plus the wish to do a story different from the official versions dished out in handouts, made her decide to talk to them alone, and she began her questioning.

The young man explained that he was trying to get this lady's case heard and get the organisers to give her a slot. But they had not applied before and it had not been scheduled, so she was not getting a chance to speak.

Gulnar Narrates:

She was married into a family of eleven male cousins, all of them living in one extended family under one roof. On reaching marriageable age all brothers were married and their wives came from far-flung villages. Special care was taken to bring girls from remote regions, and particularly from poor families. They themselves were fairly well-to-do, owning and running small shops, and also possessing land that was enough to provide grains and vegetables. The family owned several buffaloes and there was no shortage of milk and butter. The family was constantly being praised for living an austere life, contributing to the mosque and other community welfare programmes, being humble and charitable, and more than that, bringing in girls from poor families where parents could ill afford to even marry their daughters, let alone into such a well-to-do family. The women were never physically abused or tortured—most of them got on well with each other and could be seen laughing and joking, fond of each other's children, cooking and taking care of the house with love and care, respectful to the elders and caring for the menfolk.

It appeared such an ideal situation that no one questioned, noticed or observed anything.

As Gulnar began revealing, the wives were being circulated as if in a game of musical chairs. Every five or six years, the men would divorce their wives. The wife would continue to live in the house, with another family unit during her iddat. She would then be married off to another cousin, who was either unmarried or had conveniently divorced his wife.

"Didn't they inform their own families?" Zainab asked the obvious question.

"They did, but remember their families were very poor. Parents were satisfied that their daughters never came back to them as divorcees or even during the iddat. That is why such care was taken to bring girls from far-off villages and from poor families. Moreover, good looking girls were selected."

"What about the local maulvi who must have prepared the divorce papers and seen to the other details?" That was Zainab's next, obvious question.

"Oh he was hand in glove with the family that gave such huge donations for religious functions and the mosque. Anyway all this was legal according to Islam."

"What about the children? Surely patriarchy promotes the 'only mine' complex."

"All went with the common surname to school, so no questions were asked. The birth certificates had the name of the respective biological fathers."

So what did she want? What had brought her here?

She had refused to accept the arrangement. First of all, she had wanted to know the reason for her husband divorcing her. She had two sons, so it couldn't be because she was barren. She was always under the eye of the family elders and never ventured out alone. So it couldn't be 'adultery' or doubt cast on her character. All the elders loved her and she cared for them, so disobedience, bad manners or neglect could also not be cited. No proper reason was forthcoming and so she went to the maulvi. She hoped that he would speak to her husband and her in-laws who had suddenly begun to keep a distance from her. The maulvi asked her to quietly accept what she was getting—her meher, and get on with her iddat. What if she refused? The maulvi then explained to her the arrangement. Two such divorces and nikahs had taken place since she had come to this house some eight years back.

Gulnar refused to accept things. She took her dower and went to her parent's house, with the sole intention of making this perverted arrangement and legal prostitution public. She had studied till class 12, a fact that had been hidden from the boy's family, because they only wanted girls who were knowledgeable about the *Quran*. She had also been twenty-three at the time of her marriage, again something hidden from the boy's family, because they had wanted a girl who was only sixteen or seventeen years old. Armed with these two weapons she was willing to wage a war. She only needed a bit of support. She knew she would be comfortable in her new husband's portion of the house; he would not mistreat her nor would he be tightfisted about money. Her children would be right there before her eyes. Her new husband would never stop her from spending money on her children and she would be able to treat the children of her first marriage on par with the ones who came from the new one. Her sisters-in-law tried to make her see reason. After all, they had all gone through this and were quite happy with the arrangement. But all she could see was the sheer injustice meted out through religion, in God's name. She would fight it out and she would win.

She did not get a chance to fight anything. The maulvi refused to budge from his position, and the men of the family, having had their way with so many women, were hardly going to bow down to her. Her own family tried to make her see the sense in accepting the way things existed. Within a year-and-a-half she was back to the family, married to one of the cousins and then divorced after a few years and married back to her original husband.

Or maybe not the original husband, maybe another of the cousins. How did it matter?

The meeting held by the Bharatiya Muslim Mahila Andolan (BMMA), in Muradabad, proved to be a catharsis of sorts for the two-dozen odd victims of mental violence—namely Halala and Triple Talaq. "Many who went through this could not gather enough courage to come out and face the world," said the BMMA president, Naish Hasan.

A couple of years ago, Naish Hasan had created ripples in conservative Lucknow by dashing off a letter to the octogenarian president of the All India *Muslim Personal Law Board*. She demanded the inclusion of women's issues on the agenda in its next executive meeting. Her demands included a ban on Halala and Triple Talaq, apart from recommending a codification of the Shariah to avoid misinterpretation. "The response from AIMPLB, was as anticipated—nil to date," says Naish.

In her letter, she mentioned seven victims who were subjected to Halala an excruciating two to eight times. One of them was Hanifa Bano, whose husband literally turned her into a prostitute. "He would pronounce 'Talaq Talaq Talaq' when drunk, when annoyed, when fired from his job, when clubbed by the beat constable or when I stopped his mother from hitting me with a ladle," she says. "Any occasion was good enough to boot me out."

Hanifa recollected that after every Halala, her husband would weep, standing alongside their children. "I bore Halala seven times. It's a terrible feeling to walk down the road, knowing that everyone in the mohalla keeps a count of your moles and curves," she says, teary-eyed. For women like Munni, whose brother-in-law volunteered for Halala, the situation was even more humiliating. "Imagine facing him every day and pretending to be normal," she said.

Contrary to the popular belief that Halala is confined to the rural belt, Naish claims that she has listed eleven such cases in the last two months in Lucknow alone. "However, women in the city are turning rebellious," she says, "Some of them have walked out of the marriage after Halala was ordered—in fact, one woman begs in the Imambara as she believes that begging is more respectable than getting raped every sixth month."

The number of Halalas is on the rise, confirms Kamaal Khan, a Lucknow-based journalist. Interestingly, Halala is also fraught with risks for the men now. There are instances where the second husband has violated the terms of a fixed Halala and refused to part with the woman—often because she was prettier than his own wife. "So caution is the keyword now," claims Kamaal, who is making a documentary on the practice, and has even recorded details of a Halala service run by maulvis in Ghazipur and Faizabad. "The cleric in Akbarpur has inherited a lucrative business from his father. He conducts the marriage and divorce ceremonies. The business is growing," says Kamaal.

According to Khan, Halala-fixing is nowhere mentioned in Islam. The provision is made for *ittifaqan talaq* by the second husband—meaning the woman can remarry the first husband if the second husband genuinely divorces her and the move is not carried out under a well-calculated strategy. "Yet it is accepted and no voice is raised against it. The way it is followed today, the practice is totally against the spirit of Islam and humanity," he says.

The astounding face of patriarchy is that for every outcome it is the woman who is held responsible and declared guilty, even where she is completely helpless or even a prisoner. In a discussion with Muslim scholars, Azghar Ali Engineer had pointed out that since it was Triple Talaq, pronounced in one sitting, that was to blame for Halala, the best thing would be that it should be done away with. It might at least lessen the incidents of Halala, if not completely stop them.

Quick came the response from another scholar, "But the system of Triple Talaq came into existence because of women." Then seeing our non-plussed expressions he gave us a superior smile and narrated the following incident:

'As you all know it was Hazrat Umar, the second Caliph and close associate of the Prophet, who allowed the practice of Triple Talaq and made it legal and binding. Haykal, in his book, explains why Hazrat Umar was constrained to enforce triple divorce despite the Quranic injunction contrary to it. Muhammad Haykal says that when the Arabs conquered Iraq, Syria, Egypt, etc. the women prisoners from these regions were brought to Mecca and Medina. These women were very attractive and charming and the Arabs were captivated by their beauty and wanted to marry them. But these women insisted on the men giving irreconcilable divorce to their former wives. To satisfy them these men would pronounce

Triple Talaq and pretend to having divorced their wives for good—then marry these beautiful women but also keep their wives.'

So these poor women, taken prisoners by the enemy conquerors, separated from their own home and country, brought to a strange land as objects of pleasure, were fooled in the first instance by Arab men, who only wished to enjoy them and not give them the respect and dignity of a wife. Till today, fourteen centuries after the incident, they are held responsible for being the instrument that made Triple Talaq possible. These women should not have insisted on a proper, legal status; they should have just agreed to sleep with the Arab men. It was they who had been unjust to the Arab men; so do the Muslim men, anywhere and everywhere, have the right to be unfair and unjust to women today—just as every woman has to be punished for Eve having tempted Adam into committing the 'original sin'? Naturally a decision taken by Hazrat Umar, under duress, and primarily to protect the captured women, cannot be overturned today. What perverted logic!

Chapter - 11

Mut'ah Or Legalised Prostitution?

Bilquis was talkative and had no qualms in talking about herself. She waved her mother away when she would interfere and shrugged her shoulders when a male shadow behind the curtain was pointed out to her.

"It is Abba, my father. He likes to be in the know of things," she sneered. "He does not matter," she said matter-of-factly when Farhat seemed to feel a bit awkward. "You have come to talk to me and you shall."

"It seemed different, the wedding. No *dholak*, no singing and no relatives—no food being cooked on a large scale and no clothes being prepared for the bridegroom. But then Abba was a staunch Muslim and did not believe in spending a lot of money in lavish marriage celebrations. Actually, I did not really care. At sixteen, it was enough that one was getting married, that my father had selected the bridegroom and that he was rich. There was ample proof of his riches, because he had sent down beautiful clothes and quite a few gold ornaments. There was also some cash that Ammi put away in her cupboard.

"Anyway, I was dressed in the wedding finery and the bridegroom's party, a group of six including the maulvi, arrived on the dot. The maulvi came to me straightaway and asked me to repeat after him. It was then that I realised that something was not quite right. The marriages of all my friends and cousins that I had attended had a different sequence. The maulvi went first to the bride's father and asked him if he had his permission to initiate the nikah, then asked the bridegroom and, after receiving a reply in the affirmative, he came to the bride and asked her whether the boy and the terms of the nikah were acceptable to her. Why did this maulvi come to me first? I looked at my father and he nodded to me, asking me to repeat what the maulvi was saying. I was alert and looked up again at the word 'mut'ah'. Abba nodded again and I thought the maulvi had mispronounced the word nikah because he had no teeth. I repeated the Arabic words, saying mut'ah, hoping that the maulvi would correct me. When he didn't I just assumed that he did not wish to be laughed at for his lisp. Then the maulvi walked up to the man who was to be my husband, who did not repeat anything, only said, 'I accept.'

"That was it. Everyone ate some sweets and drank some tea and I was bundled into a car and we drove away. My father just patted my head; neither he nor my mother seemed unhappy at losing their eldest child. I thought it must be because they had been really worried about my marriage and were relieved that I was now married into a well-to-do family. I did think though that my mother could have made a show of weeping, for sake of decorum. But I was really flying a little in the air. I was not worried. The man I had been married to was quite a bit older but good looking and well dressed.

"I was quite happy at my husband's house, though I missed my parents and my younger siblings. It took me about a week to realise that this was not my husband's family home but a house that he had bought for me. There were two servants who took care of household chores and a maid for me. Though relieved that I would not have to deal with a mother-in-law and other relatives, I was curious about his family. Because of a separate establishment I had almost no communication with the outside world. My husband did take me out shopping a couple of times and a few times to the cinema, but he was also absent for two or three days sometimes.

"Three months had passed and I had become quite confident of my position. I was planning to ask my husband to take me to his ancestral home and introduce me to his family. How did it matter if he had other wives? I must get to know them and they me.

"My husband had twice arranged for me to be escorted to meet my family. I had stayed the whole day but had to come back in the evening. Apparently my husband had not permitted a night stay. Three months and eight days had elapsed since my wedding and nobody from my family had visited me. On that day I heard my father's familiar voice at the gate. I had rushed out to greet him but he was busy discussing something with the older one of the male servants. Beside him lay two iron trunks and a suitcase. What could be happening? Had my father decided to move in with me and my husband? But how could he? What was to happen to my mother and siblings? My husband would never permit it, whatever be the circumstances.

"I did not get a chance to question my father. He saw me and without even an inquiry into my well-being asked me to pack everything that I possessed into the two trunks and suitcase. He laid special emphasis on 'everything', repeating it thrice. I asked what was the matter and was told that I had to return to my parents' house. I refused, demanding that I speak with my husband. My father replied that he was not my husband anymore. So had he divorced me? 'No,' came the reply, but my marriage was over. How? why?—the questions were left suspended in the air with my father's curt, 'all that shall be explained later; just begin to collect your things'. The elderly servant followed me around, helping me pick up my belongings, instructing the maid to fold my clothes properly. He silently removed from my hands the cut glass vase that I liked to fill with roses from the garden. It belonged to the house and had not been gifted to me.

"I was done in a couple of hours, and by afternoon was back with my family. But I refused to eat or drink anything, nor would I let anyone break a morsel, threatening to destroy everything breakable in the house till things were explained to me.

"There was nothing much to be explained. I had been married for a hundred days; at the end of which my marriage stood dissolved without a divorce. I still had to undergo the period of iddat, just in case I had conceived. Not a chance of that though. My mother had advised me to be on the pills from the menstrual cycle before I got married. Both my mother and father had planned it well—my sale!"

"So now what?" Farhat asked tentatively.

She laughed out aloud. "There have already been five more 'now whats' since that first one. Yes my dear, I have been married six times and soon there shall be the seventh one. Once it gets known that a woman has been through a mut'ah, that she is available for this arrangement, a proper marriage is no more an option that she can exercise."

"Have you tried? Have you explored?"

"You think I have not? That I am happy with this makeshift arrangement? But no one is willing to marry me for keeps now. They all suggest mut'ah right in the beginning of the discussion.

But things are not that bad. I am twenty-nine years old now and leave nothing to be settled and decided by anyone but me. I am good looking and my mother is a good masseur. It is in her interest to keep my body soft and supple. I am the family provider. My younger brothers are being educated through my money and a sister has just been married. I have a comfortable bank balance and have just bought myself a flat. I cannot be called a woman of loose morals, as everything is perfectly Islamic and legal."

"But just suppose you conceived—what then?"

"In spite of the pills I became pregnant twice. Both the times my 'husbands' arranged for the abortion. Who wants to maintain a child from a temporary marriage, and who wants a woman with a child from an earlier temporary marriage? So not having a child works well both ways. No encumbrances."

THERE WAS an ancient practice amongst the Arabs that a man and a woman could commit to being husband and wife for a specified period. Mut'ah is the Islamisation of this tribal tradition that allows a short-term marriage.

Analysts of sociology suggest that the initial marriages must have taken place when a man and woman declared themselves bound to each other through an act of intercourse in public. This was like a 'hands off' message to other eligible men and women. Even today, there are several tribes where the consummation of marriage before witnesses is considered the seal on the verbal declaration. Such an arrangement existed amongst the ancient Arabs and it was prevalent even at the time of Prophet Mohammad.

Nikah al-mut'ah is a type of marriage used in Shia Islam, where the duration of the marriage and the dowry must be specified and agreed upon in advance. It is a private contract made in a verbal or written format. A declaration of the intent to marry, and an acceptance of the terms are required just as they are in a normal nikah.

The bride-to-be must be a Muslim or belong to *ahl-e-kitab* (people of the book)—that is Christians, Jews or Zoroastrians. She should be chaste and 'not be addicted to fornication', and she should not be a young virgin (especially if her father is absent and cannot give his consent). The last is supposedly a precaution for protection of orphan girls, or girls in the care of relatives, so that they are not pushed into prostitution.

At the end of the contract, the marriage ends and the wife must undergo iddat. The iddat is intended to give certain paternity to a child should the woman become pregnant during the contract.

Generally, the nikah mut'ah has no prescribed minimum or maximum duration. It could be for several years, a few months, a couple of days or even for a few hours. However, some sects insist that the marriage duration must be at least of three days, while a period of three months or one year have been suggested as desirable.

In recent memory, the short-term marriage or mut'ah was revived by Nawab Wajid Ali Shah of Awadh. The Nawab was fond of women and was also a staunch Muslim. Since Islam does not allow more than four wives at a time, he revived the mut'ah which does not specify the number of women one can have a temporary marriage with.

The Shia sect has tried to propagate and logically uphold this custom, claiming that this was a process of legalising the sexual need of the Muslim soldiers during wars. Being away from home for long periods, these soldiers would indulge in adultery and also leave their offsprings uncared for. Thus mut'ah came into being as a safeguard for such women and children.

This explanation is totally without any factual support. Who can believe that the sex-starved soldiers of a plundering army would have the time to select a woman, discuss with her and her guardians the terms and conditions, call a maulvi and have a mut'ah?

Mut'ah was indulged in by several 'sahaba' or companions of the Prophet. Today there is a panel of advisors and helpers who answer queries of young men and women, help them find partners and also conduct the ceremony of mut'ah.

The advice given by the scholars and maulvis for an inquiry on what is mut'ah:

'Firstly we would advise you to get acquainted with the background of mut'ah and its Islamic legitimacy. There is no substitute for reading the actual texts available and the analysis that has been given about it. Only when you are convinced that it is indeed a legitimate option in Islam and acceptable in the eyes of Allah should you proceed further in this direction.'

Mutual understanding and agreement is a must for mut'ah to take place.

'Once you are aware of what mut'ah is, its legitimacy, and the commitment that it entails on both sides, it is time to discuss the terms and conditions with the person with whom you intend to enter the contract. The two people need to know each other's mind and be comfortable with the demands being put forward by each other.'

A mut'ah contract is a new one every time because the conditions and demands may differ.

'Once both parties have mutually agreed that they would like to enter into a mut'ah contract, certain things have to be further discussed and finalised. The first is the time period for which your mut'ah marriage will last; secondly the amount of meher or the dower, and thirdly any other specific condition one of the partners may wish to put down.'

The last one usually is individual specific and can range from the amount of housework and pocket money, to the number of times physical contact may be established.

The most important thing that has to be decided and put down in the contract is the time period. This should be clear, because as soon as the time runs out, the two are no longer 'halal' for each other unless they renew the mut'ah and repeat the procedure.

The meher or dower is the gift that the man gives to his wife as part of the contract. This too must be clearly recorded. Most maulvis have been known to advise their clients that they should not be extravagant in meher. As example they cite the Hadith—that some of the companions of the Prophet would enter into mut'ah with a handful of dates or wheat as the meher.

Any other condition agreed upon should also be put down in the contract and once the couple agree to the conditions, it becomes obligatory for them to abide by them.

Having finalised the above mentioned conditions and understood the requirements, both parties—the man and woman, are now ready to recite the Arabic formula of words, which, once completed, means that they are now 'halal' for each other in the eyes of God and the Law of Islam. This procedure can be done by the two persons wanting to enter the mut'ah marriage themselves. There is no need for a *wakeel*—someone who recites the 'seegha' (an oath/undertaking/verbal contract) on your behalf nor the need for witnesses. However, the parties are free to opt for a *wakeel* and also have respectable people as witnesses if they so wish. It is advisable to put this procedure in writing with the signatures of both, the man and the woman. However, these are options available to both partners but they are not necessary for the mut'ah to be valid.

The seegha is quite short but must be recited in Arabic. On

the internet one can find the Arabic formula written in English transliteration, along with its meaning. There is also a link to an audio file with the vows for the mut'ah marriage recited in Arabic. It has been recited slowly with gaps, so the parties can repeat after it if they wish to, and believe that saying the seegha in Arabic would somehow make their mut'ah more valid or the vows more holy.

The lady says:

'Zawajtuka nafsi fil muddatil ma'loomati 'alal mahril ma'loom.'

Which translates into: "I marry myself to you for the known period and the agreed upon dowry."

The man replies:

'*Qabiltu.*'

Translation: "I accept."

The word mut'ah literally means joy. It can apply to marriage—the nikah mut'ah, or to Hajj (the obligatory pilgrimage)—the mut'ah of Hajj. It is a sensitive area of disagreement between those who follow Sunni Islam and for whom nikah mut'ah is forbidden, and those who follow Shia Islam, for whom nikah mut'ah is allowed. Shias and Sunnis do agree however that in the initial years of Islam, nikah mut'ah was a legal contract. But in later years it was given up and made *haraam*.

The Shias give arguments based on the *Quran*, Hadith, history and moral grounds, to support their position. According to them, the word of the *Quran* takes precedence over that of any other scripture.

In a Hadith it says that once Ali bin Yaqtheen asked Musa al-Kadhim, the seventh of the twelve Imams, about nikah mut'ah.

The Imam inquired, "Why do you ask, when you, Ali, with the blessing of Allah, have a wife at your side?"

Ali is said to have replied, "I just want to know."

Imam Kadhim replied, "The permissibility is present within the Book of Allah."

Thus, the *Quran* itself permits mut'ah.

The Hadith also records the use of nikah mut'ah during the time of Abu Bakr, the first Caliph, close companion, and the father-in-law of Prophet Mohammad. Asma was another daughter of Abu Bakr (573 - 634 CE). She was given in nikah mut'ah to Zubayr ibn al-Awam, another sahaba, and had children with him.

It is described by Ibn Hajar Asqalani (1372 1448 CE (852 AH)) in his commentary on the work of Sahih al-Bukhari—that Muawiyah (602 - 680 AH), a medieval Sunni caliph, entered into a nikah mut'ah contract with a woman from Ta'if. She was a slave who was owned by a man called Banu Hazrmee. She received an yearly stipend from Muawiyah.

The scholar, Abd ar-Razzaq as-San'ani (744 CE), described how Saeed bin Jabeer Jubayr frequently visited a woman in Mecca. When he was questioned about this, he replied that he had a contract of nikah mut'ah with her and seeing her was 'more halal than drinking water'.

Later, in 16 AH (637 CE), Umar, the second Caliph and also a close companion of the Prophet prohibited mut'ah. For this reason the Sunnis do not allow it. Shias allege that Umar's prohibiting it was a challenge to Mohammad.

Other relevant Hadiths include those of Imran ibn Husain and Abdullah ibn Abbas. The opinion of Ibn Abbas is cited in *Fatih al-Qadir* where he has said, "The verse of mut'ah was an order and it is halal."

In the sixteenth century, during the reign of Akbar, the third emperor of the Mughal Empire, who was a Hanafi Sunni, debates regarding religious matters were held weekly on every Thursday. When discussing nikah mut'ah, Shi'ite theologians argued that the historic Sunni scholar Malik ibn Anas supported the practice. On the basis of this they managed to make it legal during Akbar's reign.

The Hanafi school of Sunni jurisprudence argues that

although the nikah mut'ah contract itself is valid, but since marriage is regarded as a permanent condition, therefore, the temporary element of the contract makes it void.

The 20th century Sunni scholar, Waheed uz-Zaman said,

"On the topic of mut'ah, differences had arisen amongst the Sahaba, and the *Ahl'ul* Hadith, and they deemed it to be permissible, since mut'ah under the Shariah was practised and this is proven, and as evidence of permissibility they cite verse 24 of Surah Nissa as proof. The practise of mut'ah is definite and there is consensus on this. The proof is definite and cannot be refuted."

The *Gharab al Quran*, the dictionary of Quranic terms, states:

'The people of Faith are in agreement that mut'ah is halal; other than them scholars of Islam, including the Shia, believe mut'ah is halal today as it was in the past.'

The *Tafsir Haqqani,* a critical explanation of the *Quran*, states,

'Some Sunni scholars deem mut'ah permissible, in the same way the Sahaba Ibn Abbas and Imran bin Haseen deemed it permissible.'

They say, 'The verse of mut'ah appears in the *Quran* and no verse has come down to abrogate it. So it stands as permissible.'

Historically, Shias say that nikah mut'ah has varied in its spiritual legality, changing from halal to *haraam* and back again, over time, and thus cannot be considered in the same light as, for example, taking alcohol, which was never advocated by Mohammad, any sahaba or any other scholar in later centuries.

Ironically, the Shias do not accept the argument that nikah mut'ah is immoral because it can be used to hide prostitution.

The Four Pillars Of Mut'ah

Shia jurisprudence discusses temporary marriages with all the care it bestows upon permanent marriages. Like permanent marriages, mut'ah too has 'pillars' and 'statutes'. To the two pillars of a permanent marriage—the formula and the persons—are added the time period and the dower .

The Formula

Since it is a contract, mut'ah requires a 'declaration' and an 'acceptance'.

The acceptance is made by the man after the woman has made her declaration. His words must demonstrate that he is satisfied with the declaration. For example, he may say: 'I will accept the marriage', or 'I accept the mut'ah.' If he should say only: 'I accept' or 'I am satisfied', the contract is still valid.

The legal discussions of contracts assert that the man and woman must be 'worthy of the contract' *(ahl al 'aqd)*—this means that those who conclude the contract must be the man and woman themselves, or their representatives (wakil), or their fathers. Hence, for example, it is permissible for the father to say: 'I give my daughter in mut'ah with her agreement.' If anyone other than the above persons should conclude the contract, it is 'uncommissioned' (*fuduli*) and therefore invalid.

The Persons

A man can conclude a contract of mut'ah only with a Muslim woman or one of the 'People of the Book'. It is not permissible to engage in temporary marriage with an unbeliever or an enemy of the Household of the Prophet (*Ahlul Bayt*, ie. the Imams).

The point to be noted is that while a man can marry a non-Muslim woman so long as she belongs to the 'People of the Book', a Muslim woman cannot marry a non-Muslim man even if he is a Jew, a Parsi or a Christian.

If the man has a permanent wife, he cannot contract a mut'ah with a slave without his wife's permission. Should he do so, the contract is invalid or in abeyance, pending her permission. If the slave should belong to someone else, a mut'ah cannot be contracted without her master's permission. Several Hadith have been recorded on this point. For example, the Imam Ja'far says: 'There is nothing wrong with marrying a slave (temporarily) with the permission of her master.'

It is recommended that a Muslim man should have a temporary marriage only with a chaste Muslim woman—'chaste' (afifa) being someone who has never committed fornication, who follows the Shariah in her activities, and is honest and upright.

The Dower

The contract must mention a dower of known property, whether in cash or kind, whose amount is safe from increase or decrease. In order to gain knowledge of the property, it is sufficient for the woman to see it, but it is not necessary that it actually be weighed, measured, or counted—whatever the case may require.

The contract of mut'ah is not simply an exchange of goods, but a marriage. Hence it is important that any possibility of misunderstandings, which might arise from not seeing the dower, be removed. As for goods which are not present, it is sufficient that they be described accurately so that the woman is informed fully and completely.

There is no condition concerning the amount of the dower. But there are specified Hadiths as well as the general Hadiths which state that if the dower is not mentioned, the contract is held to be invalid.

The woman may ask for the whole amount of the dower at the beginning of the marriage. In this case, the man may not take back any of it under any circumstances, unless for some reason the contract should have been invalid from the beginning.

The two attributes 'Muslim' and 'chaste' are derived from

sayings by two of the Imams. The Imam al-Rida was asked, "Is it possible for a man to conclude a temporary marriage with a Jew or a Christian?" He answered, "I would prefer that he engage in mut'ah with a free Muslim woman." To a question about performing mut'ah, the Imam Ja'far replied, "It is permissible. So marry none but a chaste woman, for God says so."

The Time Period (Mudda)

The time period must be delineated in a manner which allows no possibility of increase or decrease. According to Imam al-Rida, he was once asked if it was possible to have a mut'ah for 'one or two hours'. He replied, "No time limit is understood from 'one or two' hours."

There is no upper or lower limit to the duration of the time period. It makes no difference if the period is extremely long or if it is so short that there is no possibility of consummation. Any time period is permissible, so long as both sides are aware of the situation and are satisfied.

Once the contract is concluded the wife receives the whole dowry, whether or not the husband consummates the marriage before the time period expires. She is entitled to the dowry as long as she places herself at her husband's disposal and does not present him with any obstacles to consummating the marriage. When the time period is over, she is freed from the obligations of the contract.

So why are young British Muslims adopting the practice now?

"It allowed us to meet without breaking the norms of Shariah. We both wanted to date, go out for dinner, see a film or go shopping and just get to know each other better before getting married. This we wouldn't have been able to do otherwise," says Lubna.

Lubna is a twenty-seven year old data analyst from Manchester.

She is a Shia Muslim, originally from Pakistan. Lubna was temporarily married for six months before committing to a full marriage with her partner.

"It's basically a contract. A direct meeting between the man and the woman is arranged, and conditions from both sides are put forward, discussed and stipulated. We stipulated the duration, and I requested an amount of cash as dower. It was simple, straightforward and didn't take long at all," Sara added.

There is a significant number of young British Muslims using a temporary marriage as a way of balancing their religious beliefs with their modern western lifestyle.

Since the union is of an informal nature, there are no official statistics to show how many temporary marriages are taking place in the UK and in other countries all over the world. But a number of senior Shia Muslim scholars and Muslim student organisations say that there has been something of a revival of mut'ah.

The mut'ah is particularly popular on university campuses and, according to Omar Farooq Khan, president of the *Ahlul Bayt* Islamic Society at Bradford University, the practice is on the increase among Shia students.

"Definitely nikah mut'ah is on the rise now due to students becoming more aware about it. Students are educated people so obviously they look around for a solution to their problems from an Islamic perspective," says Khan.

What he is trying to say is that today's youth takes care of its physical needs. While sex outside marriage is regarded as adultery and is *haraam*, *mut'ah* is perfectly legal and halal.

Not many people are willing to openly talk about it though, and it is still something of a taboo.

It has been revived because in Islam intermingling is not allowed between sexes. In places where women are getting education and are free to move around, they would like to know the man before they agree to make a permanent commitment. That is why more women are opting for it in the West.

One has only to look up the internet to discover the curiosity, questions and counter queries from people wishing to indulge in it.

However, according to Khola Hassan, a Sunni Muslim and spokesperson for the UK Islamic Shariah Council, this practice is strictly not allowed. She says it is equal to prostitution because of the time limit applied to the union.

"I have never come across a Sunni scholar, throughout history, who declares mut'ah marriage to be halal. There is no difference between mut'ah marriage and prostitution. There is a time limit on the marriage, and the meher given as a gift from the man to the woman is like the payment to a prostitute," says Hassan.

Sayyad Fadhil Milani, spiritual leader at the Al-Khoei Centre in Brent, north-west London, is widely regarded as UK's most senior Shia Islamic scholar. He has written about the mut'ah marriage in his book *Islamic Family Law.*

"At the time of the Prophet Muhammad, peace be upon him, it was practised widely, especially when men were travelling away from home on business or at war," he writes.

The Sectarian Divide

Ayatollah Milani has said: "Islam does not permit relationships like those between a boyfriend and a girlfriend. So a nikah mut'ah gives them an opportunity to get to know each other before committing themselves to a full marriage."

He admits there is a sectarian divide over the issue: "Umar ibn al-Khattab, the second Caliph of Islam, himself said that the mut'ah was lawful at the time of the Prophet but then he went on and banned it and said he would punish everyone who did it. So some Muslims (in this case Sunni Muslims) are against it because they follow the interpretation and the suggestion made by the second Caliph. The Shias say that we stick to the *Quran* and the practices of the Prophet."

Although nikah mut'ah is a Shia concept, other types of informal marriages are practised by Sunni Muslims, such as *misyar* and *urfi*.

Misyar allows a couple to live separately through mutual agreement while *urfi* is done without the public approval of the bride's guardians. Neither of these, however, has time limits as a nikah mut'ah.

Way Of Legitimising Sex

Critics of these informal marriages, both Sunni and Shia, argue that they allow a person to have multiple sexual partners and are used as an 'Islamic cover' for prostitution or the exploitation of women, with men taking on multiple 'wives' for a number of hours. In these circumstances many of the formalities and parental permissions are dispensed with.

Omar Ali Grant, a UK resident and a convert to Shia Islam, has had around thirteen temporary marriages, but argues that he was just trying to find the right person to spend his life with. He conceded they could be used as a cover for premarital sex.

But he said, "Sex is not *haraam* per se. In Islam, sex doesn't have negative connotations; It is not impure or dirty. What Islam is saying is sex has to be between consenting adults who are also responsible. Very often it is said that a temporary marriage may amount to some prostitution, but it is not that. Prostitution does occur in certain areas of Muslim society, but then again, prostitution happens everywhere," he added.

The Term Mut'ah

The Arabic dictionaries define mut'ah as 'enjoyment, pleasure, delight'. The root form, m-t signifies, 'to carry away, to take away'.

A marriage of mut'ah is referred to both in the Hadith literature and in the books on jurisprudence (*fiqh*).

The Shias hold that this particular term is the preferred name for a temporary marriage because the *Quran* itself refers to it. In the following verse, the word 'istimta', the tenth verbal form of the root m-t is translated as 'enjoy'.

'So those of them (women) whom you enjoy, give to them their appointed wages' (4:24).

The word mut'ah was more commonly used during the lifetime of the Prophet and afterwards during the time of the Shia Imams and other Muslim leaders.

In *Wasa'il al-shia*, (the comprehensive and definitive reference work for Shias, concerning all branches of jurisprudence), the word mut'ah is employed in the headings of all sections on temporary marriages.

In some works a special term is applied to women who participate in mut'ah—*musta'jara*, or 'rented woman'. Mut'ah is considered a kind of 'rental' because a man's basic aim in this kind of marriage is the sexual enjoyment of a woman, in return for which the woman receives a certain amount of money or property.

In defining 'rental', the jurisprudents say, 'It is to gain possession of a benefit in exchange for a specified sum. Many Hadith have been recorded in which the word *musta'jara* is employed.

If a woman who has concluded a contract of mut'ah should separate from the man before the end of the time period, whether before or after consummation, the man can reduce the dower in proportion to the amount of time by which the time period has been reduced—provided that he has not already paid her the full dower.

The Imam Ja'far was asked if it was permissible to hold back part of the dower if the woman failed to put herself at her husband's disposal. He replied, "It is permissible for you to hold back what you can (ie. what you have not already given her). So if she goes back on her word, take from her the amount (in proportion to) the time of the contract broken."

However, if the woman should fail to allow the man his conjugal rights because of a reason sanctioned by the Shariah, such as menstruation or 'fear of an oppressor', then the dower may not be reduced. A man came to the Imam Ja'far and said, "I concluded a contract of mut'ah with a woman for one month for a given amount. But the woman only came to me for part of the month, and part she stayed away." The Imam replied, "An amount should be held back from her dower equivalent to the amount she stayed away from you, except for the days of her menstruation, for those belong to her."

If the woman should die during the period of the mut'ah, even if it be before consummation, her dower may in no way be lessened.

The conditions that have to be fulfilled for a mut'ah to take place give all power to the father or male head of the family in case of a minor girl, as in the case of Bilquis. Both economic status and caste play a very important role too. A man from a rich, upper caste background might desire a girl from a lower social strata. He does not wish to be encumbered with a wife from that class or have children from her who would share his name and inheritance. So he pays an amount to the girl's guardian, has a mut'ah for as long as he desires, and then walks away without having to pronounce even the Triple Talaq.

In India too, mut'ah is on the rise. Men working away from home, especially those who are employed in the Gulf, come home after long gaps. In the Gulf they lead celibate lives. Back home for a month or so, they do not wish to have a permanent wife or start a family. It is much easier to spend a small amount on the mut'ah and then be free to just leave. The woman is neither a divorcee, nor a widow, nor separated; she is just free again with a permanent tag of being available for another buyer as Bilquis stated.

The local maulvis play an important role in arranging mut'ahs. They keep a tab on both the availability of the girls and the financial conditions of their family. They also know of men who would be coming back from lucrative jobs for short periods. Sometimes the men or their families themselves contact the local maulvi and inform him of the requirement and the amount that would be offered to the girl. After keeping a commission for himself, the maulvi fixes up with the girl's parents. The girl is usually put on contraceptive pills a month before the mut'ah takes place. So there is no problem of a child being conceived. If the girl becomes pregnant there are private clinics where abortion can be performed.

A pregnancy test these days needs only forty-eight hours. But no maulvi, or even the *Muslim Personal Law Board* is ready to concede this time to the woman and allow her to get on with her life after the dissolution. A woman has to go through a period of iddat just as she would if her husband died or divorced her.

Socicty, that looks down on women who have been through several mut'ahs and misyars, in no way checks the male guardian for putting up a girl in his care for sale. Once the girls learn the facts and understand that this is what life is always going to be for them, they quickly begin negotiations themselves, open their bank accounts, transfer money to permanent holdings like immovable property and try to squeeze more and more from the man during the partnership.

But old age is a lonely time.

Saaliha is now sixty. Her last mut'ah, that lasted for just a fortnight, on the terms that she would be given three meals a day and four sets of clothes was almost five years ago. She had not managed to save anything from the nineteen times that she was in a mut'ah. What she had saved was spent on her own upkeep. Once her family realised that she was not willing to part with what she earned, they began charging her for every cup of tea that she consumed in the periods of iddat when she had to live with them. Saaliha now works as a domestic help. All her life she was told not to do any work because it would spoil her hands, her skin, her body. She is also used to good food, good clothes, cosmetics and is fond of outings and music. All these were the requirements of the earlier mut'ahs because she was expected to accompany her temporary husbands to parties. She was also expected to manage the parties they arranged to entertain their friends. She enjoyed doing that but was also aware that another woman would soon replace her.

Not used to hard labour, she is often lax in her duties and is severely scolded and mistreated and her mut'ahs are thrown at her face making her out to be a woman of loose morals. She has no children to support her or bring her some joy; she has no one in the families she was married into, since they treat her as an interloper and an outsider. As time passes she has to accept the proposal of any man, and her negotiating power becomes less and less. "What is this life but that of a prostitute?" she asks.

Massarrat agrees with her. "It is prostitution and nothing else. But it has been given a different name. It is true that a prostitute is not born; a prostitute is made. I was born in a good family, which should never have entertained the proposition for a mut'ah. The man should have been beaten black and blue by my father, my uncles and my siblings. But the money offered was huge and my father had five more children. He was not working and land holdings had shrunk with time and divisions. This was an easy way out. Rather than marry me to a factory worker or a small-time shopkeeper, he decided to have a rich temporary son-in-law. They are still very good pals, my father and my temporary husband."

"The man gets away with murder and the woman still has to abide by the laws laid down by the *Quran*, Hadith and Sunnah," says Nasreen, turning the shami kebab with the spatula. Nasreen is the fortunate one. She had been older and divorced, with two children, when a mut'ah was proposed. Knowing that this was the best that would be offered she had agreed. In the first week she had bought a shop in a new housing complex. By the time the mut'ah was over she was ready with an eatery that opened for lunch and remained open till midnight. "We Muslims know how to cook and this place soon got a name for itself. Now I employ six boys who help in the supply, preparation and packing. Soon I plan to have another outlet somewhere in the centre of the town." Nasreen does not depend on anyone, takes care of her two children, lives comfortably and is expanding her business. But for Saaliha and other women like her, mut'ah is the legality with which men assuage their conscience while treating women as commodities that can be bought and discarded.

Perhaps Nasreen is the answer to the desperation and destitution that leads women and their families to resort to mut'ah. Economic independence of a woman will bring security, and hopefully lead to social self-reliance as well. But that is a long way away, and the abuse of women through religion will continue unless it is checked. The answer lies in the awareness and sensitisation of the community. This alone can, in the long run, bring about the required change in the thinking and mindset of people. Meanwhile, draconian laws that have been lying dormant for decades and even centuries, are being revived, quoted and brought into use.

As an example, one has to only look at the laws that have been brought in by the Taliban and followed in areas of Pakistan. A glaring example is the imposition of the 'Jizya Tax' on the non-

Muslim population in regions that came under Taliban rule. Jizya had been non-existent since the time of Akbar in Asia. Aurangzeb had tried to revive it but had failed miserably. In the last four centuries, a policy of mutual respect and brotherhood had been practiced by the Mughal rulers in Delhi, and other Muslim feudal lords, with the Hindu, Christian and Sikh population.

The Amirs of Kuwait, Saudi Arabia and Qatar too had never thought of reviving it. Iran had done away with it more than three centuries back. All of these countries are ruled by Muslims and governed by the Shariat. But the Taliban imposed the 'Jizya Tax' in Afghanistan. Swat Valley was quick to follow and now Pakistan occupied Kashmir is also said to have levied this tax. The Sikh and Hindu populations, who were at the receiving end of this injustice, began migrating, mostly to India and a few to the west.

Jizya is nothing but protection money, paid to local goons who in turn pay it to the don of the region. It allows the non-Muslim population to practice their profession or continue their trade and business. This tax is an arbitrarily fixed amount. In Afghanistan it was seen that its revival was a non-violent way of pushing the local Hindus into a position where they had no other option but to leave their homes.

So what happened after the entire non-muslim population had moved away? Were the oppressors satisfied after the cleansing? Did they then rule peacefully and with justice over the now religionwise homogenous society? Facts tell us that they did not! In Afghanistan, Swat, Pakistan Occupied Kashmir and other pockets within Pakistan, the tyrant then turned on different sects within Islam. The targets have been Ahmediyas or Qadiyanis, the Ismailis, the Shias, the Hazaras, and the list goes on.

Intolerance has become a habit. The same pattern applies to patriarchy. If women have been submitting to a pattern of patriarchy till now, they can be sure that its ring is going to get tighter. Mut'ah and *misyar* have been revived and have gained popularity over the last three decades. Triple Talaq seems to have become popular and Halala is on the rise. For women, the few reforms that had taken place from the middle of the nineteenth to the beginning of twentieth century have been carefully targeted, picked out, and removed from society. In their place, these laws have been revived, and with them, has also been revived the fear of Hell, social stigmas and religious ostracisation.

There is no way these laws can be interpreted in favour of women or to give her justice. Can the Indian society look the other way while the Muslim woman is being given such a raw deal? The answer lies in reaching out for a unified civil code. Ambedkar had imagined that this would happen naturally, in the course of time, as communities saw and understood its benefits. Since that is not happening, it is time to take a firm stand and make a studied, conscious move towards equalising the rights of women, as advised by the Indian constitution, irrespective of her community or sect.

Chapter - 12

Fake Talaqnamas

A group of over 200 Muslim women got out of their kitchens last on a Sunday afternoon in 2012 with a silent determination to fight for justice in their marital rights. From across Lucknow, and outside too, they came together in a cramped hall to move towards justice.

Face partially hidden by a tightly wound dupatta, Afzal Bano seemed too docile to be a revolutionary, much like the other women. The group looked near identical, especially in their body language—defiant yet unsure—that the bright salwar suits and chador could barely mask. Afzal called on the women to fight for justice. *"Hamen Musalman khawateen ke liye insaaf chahhiye* (we want justice for Muslim women)," she declared boldly, looking for assurance towards Shaista Ambar, president of the All India Muslim Women Personal Law Board.

Ambar, who broke away from the All India *Muslim Personal Law Board* to form her splinter women's group, is a known iconoclast. After launching a feminist nikahnama a few years ago, which makes registration of a Muslim marriage compulso , her followers expect her to take on the contentious issues of Triple Talaq, Halala and dowry next.

In the past five years, Ambar and her followers have helped many women like Rabia and Tina. Rabia is grateful to Ambar for having saved her from 'submitting to the indignity of Halala'. Tina, whose doctor husband pronounced talaq over the telephone, tackled the indignity via the forum.

"Triple Talaq, pronounced in a fit of rage, under influence of liquor, without observing the iddat or counselling, is against Islam," Ambar told the group and everyone nodded in unison.

"Tell this to the maulvis," said Samina. The deserted wife of an air force pilot, Samina, from Chandigarh, had been contesting a maintenance claim in the Lucknow court. Her husband had bought talaq from a local maulvi and refused to pay maintenance. But she is determined to fight on, she told the others. Reshma, Nafeesa, Fatima, Sayeeda, Naznin—the number of young wives betrayed and dumped is swelling by the minute.

Syeda, whose husband bought a fake talaqnama for Rs 500, went to a senior cleric to lodge a complaint. But his response was, "*Allah saza dega unko*" (God will punish him). The middle-aged Syeda doesn't want to wait till the death of her husband, when he shall be given a place in hell and all kinds of furies shall torture him. What about her own punishment which continues for no crime committed? "I want justice while living," she fumed, adding, "Let him cough up my meher money so my son can set up a tea stall." This fake talaqnama records that she has been paid her meher and that there is nothing due from her husband's side.

What punishment should be the fate of the maulvi who issued this fake talaqnama? While the Indian law would punish this man for forgery and the talaqnama would be declared 'null and void', the *Quran* is silent on such issues. Infact, forgery does not even figure as a crime or sin in the eyes of Allah. Having two witnesses takes care of everything.

Talaq can be performed through a letter, through email and even over the mobile. The connection might be bad, and the woman might not even understand the exact words that are said, but if the man has two witnesses, the talaq is accepted. The maulvi is ready to issue the talaqnama, and the divorce is final.

There is also a tradition of marrying the girls to the *Quran*, that exists both in Sindh and Punjab areas of Pakistan. Since women did not have a share in the father's property in these areas, Islam introduced this as a law. It evolved as the solution to the problem of dowry—almost like the Mughal kings never marrying off their daughters or sisters. How could the emperor part with one-third of the his empire?

One would wish to question the state of mind and the social attitude of these maulvis. Why is the maulvi so ready with documents and formalities? Why is he so keen to fulfill the dictates of the religion? Sometimes the fee that he charges is quite high but most of the time we know that he is paid a nominal amount—both for the divorce and for the nikah. Is he getting some sadistic pleasure out of knowing that a woman is being defiled? That religion is forcing her to go through sex that she does not want and does not desire? Why is the clergy always found on the wrong side of humanity when it is a question of women? Why haven't the maulvis, both the Barelvis and the Deobandhis, got down to making a contract, that if Halala has been conducted once it can never happen again? Why are there so many women who have been through it again and again? Why are fake talaqnamas available and why hasn't the community got down to punishing the maulvis who indulge in such practices?

Presumably, when the *Quran* was being revealed the number of Muslims was very limited and everyone knew everyone else or at least their family or clan, and so, it was just impossible to commit forgery and not be caught. But things have changed now. Not only has the count of Muslims become enormous, their sects and sub-divisions too have multiplied—each group having their own traditions, rituals and interpretations of the *Quran*. Unlike the Hindus, where one cannot change ones caste at will, Muslims can migrate from one sect to another at their convenience. One fine day a Sunni can declare that he is a Shia or vice-versa and there shall be no problem except the social or emotional one. This person can then declare the Triple Talaq or have a mut'ah as his choice.

These women are attempting to move towards a 'progressive interpretation of Shariat' to be enshrined in the Constitution, as against the chauvinistic approach of the maulvis. The message is clear in bold red on their banner, *'Aanchal jab hamara hai, parcham bhi hamara hoga'*, that roughly translates into, 'With the veil as our banner, we will fly the flag (of justice)'.

Shariat again is an interpretation of the *Quran*. It has absorbed within itself the customs and norms of the region and the times when it was formulated and finally written down. But it does not, and cannot possibly take care of the changing society and the demands of the times.

If one looks at the world map and sees the spread of Islam, one would understand that Islam, in its movement, encountered innumerable civilizations, tribal settlements, and nomadic societies. These had their own customs, traditions and laws which had evolved over the centuries. While the conquerors brought in a new process of worship and the concept of a single God, it is impossible to imagine that all social norms could, through a single stroke, be replaced by Arab (Bedouin) ones. Perhaps the most glaring example of this is the survival of Sufism—a process of 'being' and not just worship. Sufism spread from Iran to Sindh (in Pakistan). Today it is very conveniently considered to be a branch of Islam, and is credited with having made a larger contribution to the conversion to Islam than the sword.

Chapter - 13

Widows And Iddat

One of the things that is absolutely screaming to be questioned is the iddat—the waiting period for the woman.

It was early in the morning and Kaneez was rushing from the kitchen to the bathroom to the cupboard, trying to get dressed, prepare her tiffin box and catch the 7:20 am school bus. A telephone call was just not welcome, and Kaneez cursed under her breath as the popular song resonated in the small flat. Hopefully, it would be the bus driver informing her of a breakdown. It was not. The desperation in the voice at the other end alerted her and she gave it her full attention, "Nuzhat *baji*?"

"Yes it is me Kaneez. Can you come to see me today? Please, it is urgent."

"What has happened Nuzhat *baji*? Are you alright?"

"Barely. Come and I'll tell you. And Kaneez I know you like wearing a sari and a bindi, but can you please come in a salwar kameez and without a bindi."

"Why?"

"You might not be allowed to meet me otherwise!"

"What is going on *baji*?"

"Just come. Bye."

This was weird. Nuzhat Anees, the art teacher and Kaneez' colleague, was almost ten years her senior. Right from day one, when Kaneez had joined as the teacher of History, Nuzhat had taken her under her wing. Not just her, she was like an elder sister to most of the faculty. An attractive woman, she always had a joke to tell, a shoulder to offer and a couplet to recite. No one had seen her depressed or unhappy, even though most of her friends knew that she had had a fairly difficult life. Nuzhat had lost her husband about a month and a half back. He had come to her with two daughters from his previous marriage. For some reason Nuzhat's father had taken a fancy to him and accepted the proposal of a man almost fifteen years senior to his daughter. Not that he was rich or had been much of a provider. Nuzhat was a Bachelor of Fine Arts, and it was she who became an art teacher in a public school, bore three sons, got her step-daughters married and took care of the house. She was a fiercely independent woman, who refused to hear a word against her man. Did she fall in love with him or was it a façade that she had built for her own protection? He vanished from her life as suddenly as he had appeared, complaining of a chest pain early in the morning. He was gone before help could arrive.

One thing though—inspite of the complete absence of earning skills the man had been very progressive and liberal in his thinking. One of his favourite pastimes was debating the rights and the wrongs of the Islamic scriptures. He was often at loggerheads with the Muslim clergy, often disrupting Islamic congregations with his deeply researched queries. They lived in the heart of the Muslim area in the Okhla village near the Jamia Milia Islamia, and most of the points he raised were in this hub of staunch Muslims. Maybe it was this that Nuzhat admired in him—his guts to stand alone with what he believed was right. She was always by his side, and the duo had their share of admiration and condemnation from the community.

In the Soyem Majlis (a gathering and ritual performed on the third day after death), Kaneez had been rather surprised to learn that Nuzhat *baji* would be taking four months leave without pay to complete the iddat! In the two discussions that Kaneez had had with Anees sahib, he had completely rejected the idea of iddat after the death of the husband. He had written several articles informing people about the pregnancy tests that showed a pregnancy within forty-eight hours; pregnancy being the reason given for a woman to observe iddat. So why was Nuzhat *baji* taking a stand against her husband whom she had defended all the time?

Kaneez had removed the bindi but she was wearing a sari. She always attended school in a sari, and since she was visiting Nuzhat Anees on the way back from work she could do nothing about it. It was a steep staircase, and Kaneez was gathering up the sari to hold it out of the way as she began the climb when a male voice cleared the throat and asked from behind, "Going where, *mohtarma*?"

Kaneez turned and faced the man who quickly looked away. 'Never look a woman in the eye.' Kaneez smiled to herself. "I am visiting Nuzhat Anees. Why?"

"She is in iddat." The young man informed her.

"I know, that is why I have come."

"You are alone?" he inquired rudely.

"Well I cannot see anyone else around me—can you?"

"Okay go," the man said grudgingly, but stopped her before she had climbed three steps. "What did you say your name was?"

"I didn't. And shouldn't you not be asking the name of strange women? Anyway I am Kaneez Bilgirami."

The man gave her a quick 'once over'. A woman with a Syed name and dressed in a sari, going about without a burqa! Not having anything more to say, he nodded towards the staircase. "I can wait a few moments while you think of some other inquiries," Kaneez sneered.

"We have to be careful," he answered.

"Anyone would think a woman could rape another one," grumbled Kaneez under her breath as she reached up and rang the bell.

The door was opened by a maulvi whose inquiries were stemmed by "Kaneez *khalajan*! Ammi has been waiting for you!"

The maulvi made way for her and Sabir, Nuzhat *baji*'s eldest son, who escorted her inside the house to the bedroom. It was almost dark inside, and Kaneez, knowing her friends dislike for thick curtains, waited for her eyes to get used to the dim light before moving towards the contours of the figure she presumed was Nuzhat. She was suddenly engulfed in a desperate embrace; the kind that begs for solace rather than warmth or love. Hugging her tight Kaneez felt the silent jerks that she knew were suppressed sobs, kept in check for some reason she could not understand. What was the problem with a woman breaking down and having a good cry over the death of her life partner?

When Sabir left, Nuzhat got up and shut and bolted the door. To Kaneez' inquiring look she said, "We have to talk softly so that my voice does not reach the drawing room."

"Why?"

"Maulvi sahib is sitting there and he will hear it."

"So?" Kaneez was perplexed.

"But he is not my son or brother. He is a stranger, and the voice of a woman observing iddat should not be heard by a man outside her immediate family circle.

"Really *baji*...!"

"Shhh! Your voice might reach outside and they might think it is me." Nuzhat's eyes had a haunted look.

"What is going on *baji*? I can understand you observing iddat even though Anees bhai was dead against it. But what is this about 'veil of the voice'? Why were you so desperate for me to visit you, and why was I asked so many questions before I was allowed to come up?"

"During iddat I cannot have Hindu women visiting me Kaneez. I have been educated and have worked all my life in institutions where I have made more Hindu than Muslim friends. But none of them can visit me in these difficult days."

"But the *Quran* does not say this. Both of us have read it and you know this as well as I do."

"We shall talk about all that later. First help me change the bedsheet. It is so difficult to do it alone, and then do water my plants on the balcony. Most of them are dying."

"Why, no water on the second floor?"

"No silly. I have to do it after dark and I forget. The children have no time for my hobbies."

"Now don't tell me that this too is part of iddat!"

"It is. No strange male should behold my face in these four months and ten days. The sun is considered to be a male so I have to observe purdah from it too."

"Good heavens, and what about the sky! That too is a male and would behold your face in the night, and the stars, and surely the moon as well."

Nuzhat's lips quivered. She seemed close to breaking down. Cursing herself, Kaneez embraced her friend. Nuzhat soon controlled herself and said almost to herself, "Actually there is a logic in all these religious dictates. If I step out on the balcony in daylight some strange man might just see me and that would be sinful."

Kaneez could see that Nuzhat was trying to justify the absurdity of the religious rituals through logic. Holding her hand she murmured, "*Baji* you know religion does not put all these restrictions on the woman. These are the manipulations of mullahs, meant to torture the helpless. Why are you giving in to them?"

Nuzhat swallowed and then slowly it tumbled out. "Your Anees bhai was dead set against these rituals so I did not wish to observe them. But then my sons insisted saying that it was they who had to move around in the neighbourhood, and that they would not be able to face society with everyone laughing at them as the sons of a woman who did not even mourn the death of her husband."

"But Anees bhai did not believe in all this. That is a plea that you could have taken."

"He is dead Kaneez, and I have to live with my sons. How can I survive alone? I have to do what they tell me to do."

These were the sons she had worked so hard to bring up as good human beings. They knew, and had seen the labour that had gone into giving them a comfortable life and good education. Yet, when a choice was put before them, they decided to side with religion and society rather than with their hardworking, unhappy and lonely mother. As Kaneez sorted this out within herself, from somewhere arose Anees bhai's voice, answering a query she had laughingly posed to him almost seven years ago.

"Why are you always at loggerheads with religion Anees bhai? Just let it be. Let people practice it the way they want."

"If religion is left alone, and if there are no limits, no barricades constructed to check it, there is no knowing to what level it will sink. Everyone shall then be trying to prove that they are more religious than others. It can reach your friends, your family and even turn your own children against you—giving them the assurance that what they are doing is God's work and must be done."

Nowhere does the *Quran* speak about the woman observing purdah of voice or from the sun, the sky etc. Nor does it put any restrictions on her moving around freely in her house. Have these been added for harassing women in a patriarchal system, that prides itself on the religious strictness and social taboos that it forces its women to observe.

'O PROPHET ! when you divorce women, divorce them for the prescribed period, and thereafter reckon the period; and fear Allah, your Lord. And if you are in doubt as to the prescribed period for such of your women as have despaired of monthly courses, then know that the prescribed period for them is three months, and also for such as do not have their monthly courses yet. And as for those who are with child, their period shall be until they are delivered of their burden. And who so fears Allah, He will provide facilities for him in his affair.

'If any of you die and leave widows behind, they shall wait concerning themselves four months and ten days: when they have fulfilled their term, there is no blame on you if they dispose of themselves in a just and reasonable manner. And Allah is well acquainted with what ye do.'

— *Quran* 2:234

So a woman who is divorced by her husband has to wait (at least) three monthly periods, and a woman whose husband has died has to wait (at least) four months and ten days before they can marry again. The main objective appears to be that there should be no doubts as to the identity of the father if the woman gives birth to a child later on. If she turns out to be pregnant, then her waiting period lasts until the birth of the child, otherwise she is free to remarry after the three months, in case of divorce, or four months ten days in case of widowhood.

There are two exceptions stated for divorced women:

- If the woman is pregnant, then her waiting period ends with the delivery of the child.
- If the couple has not consummated their marriage, then there is no waiting period at all.

The *Quran* explicitly talks about remarriage after being divorced or widowed—that Allah prefers women to exist in nikah and not live alone. However, the women of the Prophet's family (ahl-e-bait) could not remarry after widowhood.

The Shariat has been written taking into account the *Quran*, the Hadith and the Prophet's life. The most correct way of existence might be in a nikah for a woman as per the *Quran*, yet the most pious way for a widow is to remain one always and live her life in the memory of her dead husband. Since this would be in direct contradiction to the Holy Book, it has been decided by society that the period of iddat be made as torturous and unbearable as possible.

The Controversial Question of Marriageable Age

The same can be said about the insistence of the Muslim clergy on the correct age of marriage for girls. The Indian constitution has fixed eighteen years as the minimum age for a girl to be married. Every other year the Muslim clergy is up in arms demanding that the age be lowered for Muslim girls, since the Prophet himself married Ayesha when she was only nine, and the Prophet's life is an example to be followed. Behind that is the vote bank policy of the political parties who are all out to please the clergy and the men of the community. The latest example is Kerala, where the age was lowered to fifteen years for the Muslim girls. PILs and public protests have had some effect, and the Supreme Court has taken action. The over enthusiasm of the state government to please the men of the community has been corrected; but the marriages that took place in those months have been legalised, thus providing a precedence which could be used time and again.

The Kerala government released a circular legalising the registration of marriages of Muslim women younger than eighteen years and Muslim men younger than twenty-one years, basing it on the fact that Muslims are allowed to follow the *Muslim Personal Law* in all civil matters. However, there is the Prohibition of Child Marriage Act of 2006, which makes it illegal for any Indian woman, irrespective of religion, to get married before the age of eighteen.

This circular was released by the government as a response to a query by the Kerala Institute of Local Administration (KILA), regarding the numerous complaints and legal issues faced by Muslims who were struggling to get a passport because their marriage was considered illegal. However, the circular met with widespread protests from leading feminist Muslim organisations and other political parties, who felt that it legalises marriages of girls younger than eighteen years of age, thus encouraging child marriages, which is in direct violation of the Child Marriage Prohibition Act .

Following this, a leading Indian newspaper, *The Times of India*, conducted a poll among Muslim students to see how many of them supported the reduction in marriage age. A whopping 84 per cent of women said they were dead against it. A video recording of this survey shows some Muslim girls saying that infact the legal age of marriage should be amended to twenty-one years. A woman at least gets the opportunity to complete her education, and become mature enough to choose her own life partner.

The constant discussion within the community is that too much education is a hindrance to a girl's married life, and that if the girl turns twenty, grooms shy away thinking that she has reached this age because she has some flaw or has been rejected by earlier suitors. The trend in northern parts of Kerala shows that many families have their daughters marry at the age of fifteen or sixteen, and then wait for them to turn eighteen to legally register it. The reasons cited for supporting the marriage of girls younger than eighteen is that it helps save the youth from going astray. In cases where a girl elopes, or has an affair with a boy before she turns eighteen, their marriage should be legalised as soon as possible. It is believed that the Child Prohibition Act is a hindrance against this. However, these issues or reasons are not limited to a community or religion or even region. Marrying girls in their early teens is still a practice in most parts of rural India; and yet the circular was singularly targeted at Muslim women.

After much opposition, the government edited the circular to insert an 'end date', stating that only marriages conducted before June 2013, between underage Muslim boys and girls, could be legalised. As of now, the controversies have died down.

Not only is this against the Indian constitution, it is also against Islam, where a girl has to say yes or no to a marriage proposal. It is impossible for a young girl of twelve or thirteen to realise what she is letting herself in for.

The *Quran* again contradicts itself here. It gives the right to say 'no' to the girl at the time of nikah. However in another 'Ayat', it says that the father, brother or guardian has the right to find a suitable life partner for their ward, and it is the girl's duty to obey their wishes. Thus what the *Quran* gives to a woman with one hand, it takes away with the other. In Islamic countries that are governed by Shariat Laws this is the plea taken by parents of girls who desire to marry against their father's wishes.

Momin Khan (name changed), a British-trained psychiatrist practicing in Lahore, Pakistan, has worked with teenage soldiers in Sudan and young Taliban recruits in Afghanistan and Pakistan.

He now manages the Saidu Sharif Teaching Hospital in the Swat Valley, an area that came under the spotlight when terrorists attempted to kill fifteen-year-old Malala Yousafzai because of her struggle to promote girls' education. "These girls... it's so tragic," he says. "Their families do not support them and the law of the land does not exist in the tribal regions."

Many child brides come to Momin with severe pain, sometimes blinded or paralysed—the effects of a psychiatric condition known as 'conversion disorder'. Practically unknown in the West since the beginning of the twentieth century, it has reached epidemic proportions in the tribal areas of Pakistan and Afghanistan. It is a sort of psychological stress that manifests itself in physical ailments, including convulsions, paralysis, or fits.

"Here women don't have a voice, particularly girls," Momin says. "She can't say, 'No, I don't want this marriage' ... so she keeps it all inside, and eventually it will come out in the form of some physical distress. We receive loads of women here, three to four cases with the same symptoms every day only in my clinic, and I mean daily! Thirteen-fourteen-year-old girls, all married for at least three years."

The demand in India to lower the age of marriage for Muslim girls is a step in this direction—it would see women reduced to the status of being just a commodity. A visit to any big Dargah would show that this is happening on the sly. There is always a line of devotees requesting *taveez* and *ganda* (amulets) as protection against djinns and ghosts. According to one of the *khidmatgars* at the Ajmer Dargah of Khwaja Moinuddin Chishti, more than half of the requests are for women who have fits and get hysterical for no rhyme or reason. Perhaps the number is not very high, and the cases are not confined to any one area, so support centres have so far not come up. The clergy has its own interests, the men are not really bothered and the educated Muslim women are either not organised, or do not even care.

Chapter - 14

Laws Distorted Rights Denied

Pakistan had, in its more liberal and progressive time, brought out a standard nikahnama. This has a line that gives a woman the right to divorce. According to this, she can request for a divorce without giving a reason, and obtain it without the husband permitting or agreeing to it. She also does not need to buy her freedom by paying the husband something. This is said to have come about when Mohammad Ali Jinnah, the founder of Pakistan, declared that women were equal to men. This line is still there in the nikahnama. However, it is also a standard practice that the maulvi conducting the nikah crosses out this line. The result is that the woman does not have the right to divorce, and has to go through the tiresome process of khula in case she wants a divorce.

The addition of this line to the nikahnama was a step towards giving women equal rights for continuing in a relationship or getting out of it. Had it stayed in practice, and was explained to the girls, like the rest of the conditions of the marriage, it might have become the basis for future changes in women's rights—rights that women were winning all over the world.

One wonders if the man who is marrying a woman would get really offended if the father or brother were to insist on keeping this clause in the marriage contract? Taimur Rehman of the *Laal Band* fame, insisted on retaining this line saying that he wanted his wife to have the right to leave him just as he had. But he is a progressive, educated, Leftist.

Adoption

In a landmark judgment, the Supreme Court has recently given Muslims the right to adopt a child despite their personal law prohibiting it. The apex court has said that the laws of the land have to get primacy over the personal laws of any religion, till the country achieves a Uniform Civil Code as provided in Article 44 of the Constitution.

The SC bench said that the right to adoption is conferred by a law and the following of this cannot be negated by a personal law dictate. The judgment was delivered on an eight years old petition by Shabnam Hashmi, who had approached the apex court after being refused permission to adopt.

Though the apex court said that all individuals had a statutory right to adopt a child, it also said that the time was not ripe to declare this right as a 'fundamental right'.

However, this judgment of the SC has evoked strong reactions from the *Muslim Personal Law Board.* Though the petitioner in the case, civil rights activist Shabnam Hashmi, has rejected the suggestion that the verdict sought to 'interfere' in the *Muslim personal laws* and claims that the apex court had only expanded the scope of the Juvenile Justice (Care and Protection of Children) Act.

Hashmi, who had approached the apex court to be legally recognised as the parent of her adopted daughter, Seher Hashmi Raza, said, "When we adopted Seher we were told that there was no law under which non-Hindus can adopt. So, we got her under the Guardianship and Wards Act. This verdict means that my daughter finally has legal rights. Till now, in the absence of a law, she was called my ward and I, her guardian."

Before the Court's verdict there was no adoption law for people belonging to communities other than Hindus, Sikhs and Jains. Parents of other faiths were accorded the status of a guardian and their adopted children were described as wards.

A Bench led by Chief Justice P Sathasivam ordered in its judgment: "Personal beliefs and faiths, though must be honoured, cannot dictate the operations of the provisions of an enabling statue. The personal law would continue to prevail, but in adoption case, if a member of a minority community takes recourse to the Juvenile Justice (Care and Protection of Children) Act, which is in conflict with the personal law, the Juvenile Justice Act will prevail."

A number of Muslims have welcomed the judgment. Syed Zafar Mahmood, former OSD to the Sachar Committee, and at present, president of the Zakat Foundation of India, welcomed the verdict saying, "The popular perception that Islam does not allow adoption is wrong. In fact, the Prophet encouraged adoption."

However, there are others like Hamid Kazi who say "The Supreme Court has expanded the scope of the Juvenile Justice Act. The Indian Law respecting our Shariat Law has always made me very happy.

"Reading the news of the latest Supreme Court judgment just gives a clear message to all Indian Muslims: If you do not want to follow Islamic Shariah law, you can go to the courts, and slowly but surely, we will keep on making changes in the name of Indian Law to be followed by all Indians.

"We must first look at our people who want to get the changes for their personal needs and benefits against the book of Allah. There will be so many cases filed in various courts in India like this, so we must challenge such a decision and stop it now before thousands of cases get judgment showing this Supreme Court judgment to all."

Hamid Kazi doesn't stop there. He requests his Muslim lawyer brothers to challenge this judgment and also tells Shabnam Hashmi to first 'suffer the pain of pregnancy, then have a child'—then only would she know the difference between adoption and child bearing.

He goes on to suggest that a *fatwa* can be issued against her by the muftis declaring her a non-believer for going against the Islamic law. He claims that this is very much in their hands and the social media can give this *fatwa* greater publicity than the news of the judgment. The muftis can also declare that she cannot be buried in any Muslim graveyard for being a non-believer.

The All India Muslim Personal Law Board (AIMPLB) spokesperson, Abdur Raheem Qureshi, said that it would explore legal options against the judgment as the verdict 'interfered' with the fundamental rights guaranteed under Article 25 of the Constitution.

What the people who are taking a stand against this judgment do not understand is that adoption is not the easy way out for women. In the typical patriarchal glorification of motherhood and labour pains, some men might claim that this is a painless way for the liberal, educated women to 'escape the trouble and still get the prize.' It is not. Legal adoption, even for a Hindu, is still a very long and tedious process. Adopted or natural, bringing up a child has never been easy. It involves challenges and many times personal sacrifices too. Adopting a child is not an escape route—rather it is a way of giving a home and family to a homeless orphan.

ADOPTION, AS it is done in the west, is not allowed in Islam. One cannot attribute false paternity to a child by giving him/her a family name that is not his/hers. They also cannot inherit from someone unless they have the right to inherit biologically. There is also the issue of marriage. In Islam one cannot marry one's sibling, but an adopted child is not considered as such. So paternity must be known, so as to prevent close relatives from marrying.

That being said, Islam does allow and encourage fostering of children. This differs from adoption because the child retains his/her name, inheritance rights, etc. The Prophet said, "The best house of Muslims is one where an orphan is cared for."

In the case of finding an abandoned child and adopting it, Allah says: "Allah has not assigned unto any man two hearts within his body, nor has He made your wives who you declare (to be your mothers) your mothers, nor has He made those who you claim (to be your children) your children. This is but a saying of your mouths. But Allah says the truth and He shows the way. Proclaim their real parentage. That will be more equitable in the sight of Allah. And if you know not their fathers, then (they are) your brethren in the faith. And there is no sin for you in the mistakes that you make unintentionally, but what your hearts propose (that will be a sin for you). Allah is Forgiving, Merciful." (Al-Ahzab: 4-5)

So the bottomline is that one can take in a child but the foster child cannot inherit any property from the foster parents.

In most cases, where there is only one adopted child, and the parents wish him/her to be the inheritor after their death, they have to go through the process of re-registering the property in the child's name, buying as much gold as they can, putting it in a locker in the child's name, and resort to many other tedious and often unlawful recourses. Inspite of that, the will left by the adopted parents is often challenged, leading to long drawn out court cases.

The *Quran* is silent in the case of adoption by widows, or by single women. The fact that a woman might be alone, widowed, a good human being and might wish to adopt—not just to bequeath her wealth (if she has any), but also her love, her care—and have a family that might look after her in old age and sickness, does not occur to Allah.

This is not the only problem area that the *Quran* has not explored. It is silent on so many other things as well. Suppose a man divorces his wife in a fit of anger and then regrets his decision. He cannot have a nikah with her unless she undergoes the process of Halala. Suppose neither wishes to do that. Can they then have a mut'ah for say several years, renewing it periodically, and keep doing this until death?

A husband has the right to control a wife's wealth. But what happens in the case of a divorce? Does she get only her meher? Or does she get back her paternal wealth, business and agricultural land? What if the husband has invested in business that has not done well? Will the loss be covered in the divorce settlement?

The Hadith records many incidents where Jewish or Christian women have converted to Islam. But there is total silence in case a woman wishes to convert from Islam to another religion. Does she still get her meher, the paternal property and visiting rights to meet her children? Or is she to be shunned like a man who has moved away from the 'true faith'.

Though the Hadith gives a number of examples of women from the prophet's family explaining the *Quran* to the uninitiated and converting them to Islam, there is no possibility of female priests. The clergy is all male in Islam.

Traditions and customs are being revived to take away

whatever little rights women have enjoyed till now. On 19 October 2010, 75 women on an Islamic airliner, (*Gulf Air*), travelling to perform Hajj, were deplaned at Quaid-e-Azam International Airport, Karachi, as they were not having a *mehram* or a male companion. The *Quran* does not give this kind of instruction that every woman needs a male companion while going for Hajj! An educated, healthy and mature lady is required to have a *mehram* even if he is frail, uneducated, or even mentally retarded, for there should be somebody to guard her as she is highly susceptible to molestation. And if not, she has the potential to seduce other males, especially during Hajj, where the gathering is a mixed one and opportunities in abundance. Hence, it is all the more important for her and others that she remain in the company of a male companion even if she is eighty years old.

Women are not even allowed to worship alone and they are not allowed into the mosques.

Since women are also considered less intelligent and forgetful, it is important that one male witness should equal two female witnesses before a Qazi in a court. The testimony of two highly educated females is thus equal to that of an illiterate male.

Some say that this stipulation of 2:1 applies only in financial matters. Women are not supposed to know arithmetic, to be more precise—accounting. How is it possible that someone made for sex and procreation can understand all those complicated debit/credit entries? So let that be the domain of the men.

Could Hazrat Khadija (the first wife of Prophet Mohammed), who was running a cross-country trade and business, have done so without any calculations or knowledge of arithmetic.

In the last few years, much has happened to highlight how women are being thought of in the Muslim world.

On 18 October 2010, the Supreme Court of United Arab Emirates ruled that a man has the right to punish his wife under

Islamic law, to discipline her. That includes beating her, after he has tried other options such as admonition and abstaining from sleeping with her. Beating is allowed but it should leave no scars. There are differences of opinion among various *makatib-e-fikr.* For example, the scar should not be black; if it is red it is fine. Another school of thought believes that the size of the scar should not be bigger than the size of the male fist. It can be below the neck and above the navel. Another school of thought considers beating above the navel *haraam* but below it as halal. Another considers beating the frontal area of a women's body as halal, and the rear area as *makrooh* (inadvisable), but not *haraam.*

In some earlier Islamic writings, females have been referred to as 'ploughing fields' (*khetian*). They are at the man's disposal for bearing of children. Marital rape just cannot happen, since the woman is at the man's disposal. According to the Muslim clergy, marital rape is an obnoxious concept invented by the West.

The *Quran* instructs the man that he should not have a second wife unless he is sure of treating both of them equally, and even then he must have the first wife's permission to marry another woman. Recently, a Pakistani mufti ruled that a man need not take his first wife's permission to marry another woman.

The Taliban has decided that Shias are disposable. Selecting Shia passengers from a bus and killing them is absolutely in order. Ahmediyas of course have been declared non-Muslims, so killing them is alright. Things are not that bad in India but they are slowly moving in that direction. And the clergy are more than willing to drive a wedge wherever possible.

Nowhere does the *Quran*, Hadith or Shariah mention that a nikah cannot be solemnised between a Shia and a Sunni. The two sects had come into being at the time the Shariat was written down. Had there been such a debate then, it would definitely have been mentioned in the Shariat. Till the 1980s, allegiance to a sect within the Muslim community was never an issue that could stop a social decision. As an example, there is the marriage of Kaifi Azmi (a shia) and Shaukat Azmi (a sunni). Recently, in Lucknow, a young couple wishing to get married were stopped on the day of the nikah, because they belonged to different sects. Not only were they stopped by the maulvi who was to perform the nikah, the clergy took it upon itself to talk to the parents, threatening them with dire consequences here, and a definite place in Hell thereafter. They even derided the girl's parents for not having brought up their daughter properly. Had they done so she would never have fallen in love with a boy from the wrong sect. The parents were so afraid of a *fatwa* against themselves that they asked their daughter to break the relationship. The boy and girl had no other option but to have their marriage registered in the civil courts.

The *Quran* accepts that women also enjoy the right to knowledge, but religious knowledge only. What would a woman do with worldly knowledge, as her main domain is her home?

A woman cannot divorce her husband even if he illtreats her but he can divorce her anytime, without her even doing anything wrong, especially if she gets old and loses the bloom of youth. A divorcee is also not entitled to any maintenance from her ex-husband under the Shariah, as we see in the famous Shah Bano case, wherein even utterly destitute Muslim divorcees are denied the right to alimony from their former husbands. Under extremely unbearable circumstances, the wife can seek khula, and after years of litigation can get a divorce but then would lose her right to *haqmehr*.

A woman's share in paternal inheritance is generally one-third of her male counterpart. Is the male more deserving? Males play a very important role in the household affairs and generally are the main breadwinners. Therefore, they should inherit the major share in property. Also males are more powerful and the 'powerful' should have the bigger share. Although the Indian Law now gives the girl an equal share in her father's property, the Muslim woman is denied this equality.

If a divorced or widowed woman cannot take care of young children, they can be sent to an orphanage.

The sum total of these versions, interpretations and *fatwa*s is that—at any given time, social beliefs and customs can be turned into laws with the support of the Shariat. These arbitrary decisions must be followed because women are a man's property. A man is even allowed to sell or buy women as slaves. Having fun with a slave is not even considered *zina* (adultery/rape). Men can have several; can even share them with their friends. However woe betide a woman if she is even found talking to a man; nothing less than death by stoning is her 'just' punishment!

There are eight Islamic countries in the world which have adopted Islam as an ideological foundation for their state institutions. These examples show the status of women in these countries:

On 22 May 2011, Manal al-Sharif, a Saudi woman with an international driving license, was arrested for driving a car, as official *fatwa*s issued by government clerics debar women from driving. In defiance, women drove cars all over Saudi Arabia. Two of them were summarily divorced by their husbands.

In August 2008, the 'Global Campaign to Stop Killing and Stoning Women' announced that there were at least eight women sentenced to die in Iran by stoning for convictions of prostitution and adultery.

During the Taliban's rule (1996-2001), women in Afghanistan were essentially put under house arrest, and women who once held respectable positions, were forced to wander the streets in their burqas selling everything they owned and begging in order to survive.

It is common among low-income families in most of these countries (even in India) for the groom to pay a bride price to the bride's family. The price is negotiated among the heads of the family; the bride herself or any other woman is not included in the negotiation process.

Every year, numerous women in Pakistan are subjected to domestic violence, marriage with the *Quran*, child marriage to settle blood feuds, acid throwing, and honour killing. Recently, a woman who had come to the Lahore court to say that she had married of her own free will was stoned to death by her father and brothers. She was three months pregnant. Incidentally, it was revealed later that her husband had murdered his first wife so that he could marry her. The crime had been proved and he had paid an amount as 'blood money'. The first wife's (dead woman's) family had forgiven him, leaving him free to marry the woman he loved.

Yemen has one of the worst records of child marriages in the world, with UNICEF records showing that in 2005, 48.4 per cent of Yemeni women, currently aged 20-24 had been married before they were eighteen, and 14 per cent before the age of fifteen.

In Oman and Bahrain, women's rights are severely restricted with regard to inheritance, marriage, divorce, and child custody. According to the most recent internationally sponsored study (2001), in Mauritania, three-fourths of all women between the ages of 15 and 49 had been subjected to Female Genital Mutilation (FGM).

Articles 1 and 2 of Universal Declaration of Human Rights state:

All human beings are born free and equal in dignity and rights.

They are endowed with reason and conscience and should act towards one another in a spirit of goodwill.

Everyone is entitled to all the rights and freedoms set forth in this Declaration, without distinction of any kind, such as race, colour, sex, language, religion, political or other opinion, national or social origin, property, birth or other status. Furthermore, no distinction shall be made based on the political, jurisdictional or international status of the country or territory to which a person belongs, whether it is independent, trust, non-self-governing or under any other limitation of sovereignty.

Yet, the UNO does not charge these eight countries with committing Human Rights violations with half of their human population.

Shariat courts

The present *Indian Muslim Personal Law* was drafted in 1937. It was called Mohammaden Law or Indian Shariat Act. Article 224 of the Indian constitution guarantees application of these laws as far as Muslim personal affairs are concerned. It is to be borne in mind that the *fiqh* (philosophy and analysis of Islamic Law) is not equal to the Holy *Quran*. The scholars of different times laid down the laws of Shariah according to the situation present during a particular time. It is important that these laws be amended, changed or scrapped, if new circumstances emerge. It is the need of the hour to keep the laws relevant to the prevailing circumstances.

Maulana Minnatullah Rahmani, the founding member of Muslim Personal Board as well as the writer of several books on this issue, wrote in his book *Muslim Personal Law* that the *masa'el* (problems or queries) were of two kinds—the issues which were never experienced by the previous scholars, and secondly, those which have to be deliberated afresh under the changing situations.

Maulana Rahmani elaborates :

"The time when the laws under Shariat were drafted has changed completely. The time when these laws were drafted, man was a real *Qawwam* (protector or caretaker of the woman) according to the *Quran*. He was not the receiver of the dowry or tilak or dinners from the woman's family. The woman was not aware of modern education, salaried jobs or the outside world. Today, the man has inverted or rather subverted the teachings of the *Quran* and Shariah completely. Now, he does not pay meher—instead he collects dowry from the woman not only in the form of net cash, but also demands property, automobiles etc. He grabs the salary, inheritance and belongings of the wife. He is engaged in illegitimate relations too. The divorce rate is increasing alarmingly. In Kuwait it is 37 per cent, Qatar 33 per cent and Saudi Arabia 21 per cent. In India and Pakistan, although it is 4-5 per cent but the percentage of the strained relations or disturbed marriages is over 60 per cent. In other words, every third house is affected by discord, hatred, court or police cases. The scholars (ulema) are not able to carry out counselling because the subject of counselling, although emphasised much in the traditions, has been totally neglected in the syllabus of the Madrasa."

Aleem Khan Falaki, another important scholar and advisor, had suggested that an arbitration office be established with a list of arbitrators consisting of scholars and mufties belonging to various schools of thought. The conflicting parties could choose the scholars according to their *maslak* and beliefs, and the people get their disputes solved in these offices instead of non-Shariat courts.

This was a suggestion that was readily accepted and Shariat courts came into existence. But over the years it was found that these all-men Shariat courts invariably acted against the women and in favour of men. In several cases every year, women began to appeal to the civil courts. It was also found that men often did not obey the decision of the Shariat courts which had no right or validity to punish the absconder.

In the year 2008, the Bhartiya Muslim Mahila Andolan (BMMA) decided to set up Shariat courts conducted solely by women, with an aim to redress grievances of Muslim women. It has started functioning in six or seven places in the country. The first All Women Shariat courts deal with various family issues, including marital discord, divorce, as well as property-related disputes.

"We will be functioning to mete out justice to women in the Muslim community with the tenets of the *Quran* which confers equal rights on both men and women. In reality however, women are often discriminated against by the all-men Shariat courts traditionally run by All India *Muslim Personal Law Board*," says Saeeda Jamadar, president of the court's Pune branch.

Saeeda, along with Zubeda Khatoon, BMMA's Maharashtra Convenor, forms the two-judge bench of the court in Pune, seen as part of the Alternative Dispute Resolution (DSR) mechanism in the judicial system.

The problem is the acceptance of the decisions of these courts by the ulema. As of now, they have accepted these courts, but they have retained the right to overrule any decision or order. So anything that does not suit patriarchy can be withheld and postponed till further inquiry.

One very important observation was made by a semi-literate, middle-aged Muslim woman from a village in Western Uttar Pradesh—Muneeza *bi*. The purpose of these Shariat courts was being explained to a group of women and they were being motivated to approach these courts rather than the civil courts. The argument being given in favour of these courts was that they would be free and would come to a decision much faster. Since they were headed by women they were women-friendly. Muneeza *bi* got up to speak and asked, "Are women always supportive of women? Had that been the case there would never have been any problem of mothers-in-law and sisters-in-law with the women who marry their sons and brothers. Even if the entire judiciary is made up of women, they shall function as men if their mindset has not been changed."

How very right Muneeza bi is! Women have been the pillars of patriarchy, and till this is addressed, analysed and sorted out, Shariat courts run by men or women are hardly going to make a difference.

The reason why patriarchy has survived and become stronger over the centuries is because Muslim women have never questioned it or its fallouts in an organised manner. They have never sought to be told why 'Allah' has been so unjust to them. They have never debated the laws dictated by religion, nor have they weighed the same laws with the ones being coined by a democratically elected government for women of other communities. Most importantly, they have never openly challenged the fact that changes in the law cannot lower the level of belief in ones faith.

Questioning is the key to change, and to make change an impossibility, all questions are termed as blasphemy. But it is questions that must be raised and answers demanded. This can be done only in a democracy. Let us begin to question—let us demand answers—so that law and religion can be separated; so that the Muslim women can have a life of peace, happiness and security.